Spain's Explorers in the Age of Discovery: The Lives and Legacies of Christopher Columbus, Hernán Cortés, Francisco Pizarro and Ferdinand Magellan

By Charles River Editors

Pizarro Statue in Lima, Peru

About Charles River Editors

Introduction

Posthumous portrait of Columbus

Christopher Columbus (1451-1506)

"At two o'clock in the morning the land was discovered…As I saw that they were very friendly to us, and perceived that they could be much more easily converted to our holy faith by gentle means than by force, I presented them with some red caps, and strings of beads to wear upon the neck, and many other trifles of small value, wherewith they were much delighted, and became wonderfully attached to us." – Christopher Columbus's diary, October 11-12, 1492

The most seminal event of the last millennium might also be its most controversial. As schoolchildren have been taught for over 500 years, "In 1492 Columbus sailed the ocean blue." In October of that year, the Italian Christopher Columbus immortalized himself by landing in the New World and beginning the process of European settlement in the Americas for Spain, bringing the Age of Exploration to a new hemisphere with him. Ironically, the Italian had led a Spanish expedition, in part because the Portuguese rejected his offers in the belief that sailing west to Asia would take too long.

Columbus had better luck with the Spanish royalty, successfully persuading Queen Isabella to commission his expedition. In August 1492, Columbus set west for India at the helm of the Nina, Pinta and Santa Maria. Befitting a legendary trip, the journey was star-crossed from the beginning. The Pinta's rudder broke early on, and just days into the journey Columbus' compass stopped pointing due north and started pointing to the Earth's magnetic north pole, something the Europeans knew nothing about. Columbus knew that the uncertainty of the expedition's destination made his crew nervous, so he hid his compass' "malfunction" from his crew. Additionally, after 30 days of sailing, the expedition still had not sighted land, so Columbus started lying to his crew about the distance they sailed each day, telling them they had sailed fewer miles than they actually had so as not to scare them even more.

On October 7, 1492, the three ships spotted flocks of birds, suggesting land was nearby, so Columbus followed the direction in which the birds flew. On the night of October 11, the expedition sighted land, and when Columbus came ashore the following day in the Bahamas, he thought he was in Japan, but the natives he came into contact with belied the descriptions of the people and lands of Asia as wealthy and resourceful. Instead, the bewildered Columbus would note in his journal that the natives painted their bodies, wore no clothes and had primitive weapons, leading him to the conclusion they would be easily converted to Catholicism. When he set sail for home in January 1493, he brought several imprisoned natives back to Spain with him.

Everyone agrees that Columbus's discovery of the New World was one of the turning points in history, but agreements over his legacy end there. Although his other three voyages to the New World were far less successful and largely overlooked in the narrative of his life, Columbus became such a towering figure in Western history that the United States' capital was named after George Washington and him. Conversely, among the Native Americans and indigenous tribes who suffered epidemics and enslavement at the hands of the European settlers, Columbus is widely portrayed as an archvillain.

Spain's Explorers in the Age of Discovery chronicles Columbus's life and his historic voyages, but it also examines the aftermath of his expeditions and analyzes the controversy surrounding his legacy. Along with pictures of important people, places, and events in his life, you will learn about Columbus like you never have before.

Francisco Pizarro González (circa 1471/6-1541)

"Friends and comrades! On that side [south] are toil, hunger, nakedness, the drenching storm, desertion, and death; on this side ease and pleasure. There lies Peru with its riches; here, Panama and its poverty. Choose, each man, what best becomes a brave Castilian. For my part, I go to the south." – Francisco Pizarro

If Columbus and Cortés were the pioneers of Spain's new global empire, Pizarro consolidated its immense power and riches, and his successes inspired a further generation to expand Spain's dominions to unheard of dimensions. Furthermore, he participated in the forging of a new culture: like Cortés, he took an indigenous mistress with whom he had two mixed-race children, and yet the woman has none of the lasting fame of Cortés's Doña Marina. With all of this in mind, it is again remarkable that Pizarro remains one of the less well-known and less written about of the explorers of his age.

On the other hand, there are certain factors that may account for the conqueror of Peru's relative lack of lasting glory. For one, he was a latecomer in more than one sense. Cortés's reputation was built on being the first to overthrow a great empire, so Pizarro's similar feat, even if it bore even greater fruit in the long run, would always be overshadowed by his predecessor's precedent. But Pizarro also lacked the youthful glamour of Cortés: already a wizened veteran in his 50s by the time he undertook his momentous expedition, he proceeded with the gritty determination of a hardened soldier rather than the audacity and cunning of a young courtier.

Spain's Explorers in the Age of Discovery chronicles Pizarro's life, but it also examines the aftermath of his conquest and analyzes the controversy surrounding his legacy. Along with pictures of important people, places, and events in his life, you will learn about Pizarro like you never have before.

Hernán Cortés de Monroy y Pizarro (1485-1547)

"Among these temples there is one which far surpasses all the rest, whose grandeur of architectural details no human tongue is able to describe; for within its precincts, surrounded by a lofty wall, there is room enough for a town of five hundred families." – Hernán Cortés

During the Age of Exploration, some of the most famous and infamous individuals were Spain's best known conquistadors. Naturally, as the best known conquistador, Hernán Cortés (1485-1547) is also the most controversial. Like Christopher Columbus before him, Cortés was lionized for his successes for centuries without questioning his tactics or motives, while indigenous views of the man have been overwhelmingly negative for the consequences his conquests had on the Aztecs and other natives in the region. Just about the only thing everyone agrees upon is that Cortés had a profound impact on the history of North America.

Of course, the lionization and demonization of Cortés often take place without fully analyzing the man himself, especially because there are almost no contemporaneous sources that explain what his thinking and motivation was. If anything, Cortés seemed to have been less concerned with posterity or the effects of the Spanish conquest on the natives than he was on relations with the Mother Country itself. Of the few things that are known about Cortés, it appears that he was both extremely ambitious and fully cognizant of politics and political intrigue, even in a New World thousands of miles west of Spain itself. Cortés spent much of his time in Mexico and the New World defending himself against other Spanish officials in the region, as well as trying to portray and position himself in a favorable light back home.

While those ambitions and politics understandably colored his writings about his activities and conquests, scholars nevertheless use what he wrote to gain a better understanding of the indigenous natives he came into contact with. Even then, however, what he wrote was scarce; Cortés's account of his conquest of Mexico is comprised of five letters he addressed to the Holy Roman Emperor, Charles V. As Adolph Francis Bandelier noted in the Catholic Encyclopedia in 1908, "Cortés was a good writer. His letters to the emperor, on the conquest, deserve to be classed among the best Spanish documents of the period. They are, of course, coloured so as to place his own achievements in relief, but, withal, he keeps within bounds and does not exaggerate, except in matters of Indian civilization and the numbers of population as implied by the size of the settlements. Even there he uses comparatives only, judging from outward appearances and from impressions."

Spain's Explorers in the Age of Discovery chronicles Cortés's life, but it also examines the aftermath of his conquest and analyzes the controversy surrounding his legacy. Along with pictures of important people, places, and events in his life, you will learn about Cortés like you never have before.

Ferdinand Magellan (1480-1521)

"Most versed in nautical charts, he knew better than any other the true art of navigation, of which it is certain proof that he by his genius, and his intrepidity, without anyone having given him the example, how to attempt the circuit of the globe which he had almost completed... The glory of Magellan will survive him." – Antonio Pigafetta

Ferdinand Magellan, known in his native Portugal as Fernão de Magalhães and in Spain, where he moved later in life, as Fernando de Magallanes, was unquestionably one of the more remarkable figures of the so-called Age of Discovery, a period in which Europeans spread their political and commercial influence around the globe. Accordingly, his name is often invoked alongside that of Columbus, but the nature of his achievements has sometimes been misunderstood. Magellan has sometimes been credited with "proving the world was round," since he and his crew were the first Europeans to reach Asia via a westward route. But such a claim is based on a popular misconception, referred to by historian Jeffrey Burton Russell as the "myth of the flat earth": the belief that medieval Europe had erroneously believed the earth was flat. In reality, essentially no educated Europeans of the late 15th and early 16th centuries doubted the spherical shape of the earth, which had been persuasively established by the scientists of ancient Greece – even down to Eratosthenes's relatively accurate measurement of its circumference in the third century B.C. It is also not quite true that Magellan himself circumnavigated the globe – in fact, he died in combat in the Philippines, leaving his surviving crew to complete the voyage. It is, on the other hand, certainly the case that Magellan was one of the most accomplished navigators of his time, and that he crucially charted territories previously unexplored by Europeans.

Perhaps the most important fact about Magellan, though, is that he succeeded precisely where Christopher Columbus before him had failed. While Columbus has gone down in history as the discoverer of America (for Europeans), finding a new continent was never his true goal: in fact, America came into Columbus's life as an unanticipated and troublesome obstacle on his planned journey to Asia. He had staked his career and his nautical reputation on the theory that the breadth of the body of water separating Europe from Asia was far less than most geographers had predicted. While most thought that a ship heading west toward Asia would run out of supplies long before arriving. As it turned out, Columbus was wrong and his detractors were right: the figure for the circumference of the earth first arrived at by Eratosthenes was more or less correct, and were there nothing in between Europe and Asia, sailors attempting to reach the East by the West would starve in mid-ocean. Yet as Columbus unwittingly demonstrated, there was something in between: namely, the adjoining continents of North and South America. When Columbus arrived in the Caribbean islands scattered between these two continents, he believed he was on the edge of Asia, and initially interpreted the northern coast of Cuba as a part of China. Only toward the end of his career, as he sailed along the coast of what is now Venezuela, did Columbus begin to acknowledge that he was in fact on the edge of a new continent, but in his bewildered state he associated it with the earthly paradise of Christian legend.

The dramatic story of the exploration and conquest of the Americas, carried out initially by the Spanish and later continued by the Portuguese, Dutch, French, and English, has captured the historical imagination like few others. But for the Europeans of the time, the establishment of trade routes to Asia remained the most important commercial ambition of all, and a consideration of Magellan's career helps remind us of this. He sailed forth around the same time that Cortés was beginning his initial expedition into Mexico, and he reached the Pacific around the same time that Cortés was penetrating the core of the great Aztec empire. Both fulfilled some of Columbus's ambitions: Cortés by conquering rich new empires for the Spanish crown, Magellan by establishing a westward route to the Spice Islands of the Indian Ocean. For sixteenth century Europe, the latter accomplishment was probably more important, and there is a simple reason for that. East Asia was at the time the economic center of the world; it was wealthier and more commercially advanced than Europe, and possessed luxury goods that were in high demand among wealthy Europeans. In economic terms, the opening up of new trade routes with Asia is a more significant development than the conquest of the Americas, and indeed the development of the new American colonial economies is unimaginable without the expansion of commerce with the East. For example, a large proportion of the gold and silver mined in the minerally rich territories of the Andes and Mexico did not remain in Europe – they were traded to China and India for silk, tea, spices, and other exotic commodities. The colonial Mexican economy, after the establishment of Spanish settlements in the Philippines, became a conduit for the trade of such goods between East Asia and Europe.

So Magellan, who bypassed South America on the way to the Indian Ocean, reminds us what the fundamental goal of European expansion in the 16th century actually was: access to the widely coveted riches of Asia. The settlement of the Americas may be seen to some extent as a byproduct of this larger geopolitical and economic development, which would culminate centuries later in a period of European dominance over Asia, which had for over a thousand years been the wealthier and more commercially influential continent. Magellan's story lacks the dramatic martial flair of the stories of the conquistadors like his exact contemporary Cortés, but he remains an exemplary figure for having connected the two opposite ends of the earth in a period we might think of as the first era of globalization. Moreover, although he sailed under the Spanish flag, his Portuguese origins bring home the centrality of Portuguese navigation in the processes that forged the modern world and the modern globalized economy. Often neglected because of the later dominance of Spain and England, Portugal contributed decisively to the commercial and political reorientations of the early modern world.

Spain's Explorers in the Age of Discovery chronicles Magellan's life and his historic expedition, analyzing the aftermath of his expeditions and his legacy. Along with pictures of important people, places, and events in his life, you will learn about Magellan like you never have before.

Spain's Explorers in the Age of Discovery: The Lives and Legacies of Christopher Columbus, Hernán Cortés, Francisco Pizarro and Ferdinand Magellan

About Charles River Editors

Introduction

Chapter 1: Columbus's Origins and Early Years

Christopher Columbus is one of the most famous and controversial figures in history, so it is fittingly paradoxical that very little can actually be established about his life with certainty. As an initial indication of how little history truly knows of the man, even his name is a subject of disagreement, partly as a result of his itinerant life and partly as a result of the array of reputations that have come to surround him in different parts of the world. Christopher Columbus is an adaptation of the Latinized version of his name, "Christophorus Columbus," which has become prevalent in the English-speaking world, but the name Christopher Columbus would go unrecognized in Spain and Spanish America, where he is known by the Hispanized version of his name: "Cristóbal Colón." While these two versions are the most widely used today, both are adaptations of his actual given name, which was probably Christoffa Corombo, as it would be pronounced in the local Genoese dialect presumably spoken in his family; a closer version to the original is the standard Italian Cristoforo Colombo.

There is little agreement on a common name for the famous sailor and explorer, but the question of his family's origins has also inspired a great deal of debate over the years. While his birth and early upbringing in Genoa is well-documented in contemporary materials, scholars have repeatedly claimed that his ancestors came from elsewhere. In part, this would seem to be a consequence of his status as a national hero and an object of patriotic pride in subsequent centuries. Thus, scholars have variously claimed that his family bloodline traced back to Catalonia, Portugal, and Spain, the latter two both being places where he spent formative periods of his career and which had a vested interest in claiming him more fully as a true son. None of these theories have gained ascendancy among mainstream scholars, nor has an intriguing claim that Columbus's origins were among the Sephardic Jews of the Iberian peninsula. A large part of the evidence for this claim is that Columbus was reticent in later life about his family backgrounds – and why, some scholars have contended, would he have been so reticent unless he were hiding something? And what would he be hiding if not Jewish origins, a major liability in the vigorously Catholic Spain of the late 15th century, which was in the process of expelling all of its Jewish inhabitants? Regardless, the absence of evidence surely does not itself constitute evidence, and the desire to tie Columbus more fully to one or another national or ethnic background mainly provides an index of the way his figure and voyages have been used to serve many purposes.

Those questions aside, there is little doubt that his birthplace was Genoa, and most scholarship has put his year of birth around the latter half of 1451. Genoa was an independent republic at the time, a sea port whose economy revolved around trade routes stretching in various directions across the Mediterranean Sea. In this milieu, it is not surprising that Columbus chose the life that he did. While in other parts of Europe (including Spain), a young man seeking adventure might have opted for a military career, seafaring and trade were an obvious choice in Genoa, which even had its own small colonies in the Greek islands. Columbus later claimed to have first gone to sea at the age of 10, but his first known voyages were on merchant ships to the island of Chios, a Genoese colony in the Aegean Sea which was a port of entry to the Eastern

Mediterranean, which in turn was the nearest point of arrival of exotic products from Asia.

Columbus was also born around the time of the fall of Constantinople to the Ottoman Turks, whose newly powerful empire threatened trade routes to Asia. In the environment in which he grew up, there were immediate reasons, both economic and religious, to be concerned about the new balance of power. On the economic front, for several centuries, Italian merchants had been able to travel safely to the East and bring back valuable trade goods (the most famous of these was Marco Polo, whose accounts of various Asian kingdoms Columbus read). Now, having conquered Constantinople, the Muslim Turks were dangerously positioned to dominate the highly lucrative trade with the East. Meanwhile, on the religious front, the Ottomans were now not only in control of the holy city of Jerusalem but threatening the Southeastern quadrant of Christendom via their new foothold on the European continent. Both commercial and religious leaders were beginning to call for a new crusade to reestablish Christian control in the East. For some, the rising Muslim power was a sign of the coming apocalypse, anticipating the final struggle between Christ and the Antichrist.

In any case, the economic goal of extending trade routes and the religious goal of expanding Christendom would remain intertwined in Columbus's later activities. A further effect of the fall of Constantinople was the arrival to Italy of thousands of Christian refugees from the former Byzantium, including Greek-speaking scholars carrying with them classical Greek manuscripts. By most accounts, their arrival was one of the major catalysts for the Italian Renaissance, and the new availability of scholarship would exercise an influence on Columbus, a man of extensive scholarly curiosities.

In his early expeditions, Columbus sailed as far north as the ports of Bristol, England and Galway, Ireland, and possibly even all the way to Iceland. These trips would crucially shift his orientation from the Mediterranean to the Atlantic, a sphere of travel and trade that had been unfamiliar to him when growing up. His realignment toward the Atlantic, and thus toward the West, was completed when he settled in Portugal around 1476, ironic given that Columbus started looking west as the Portuguese were fixated on looking east. His arrival in Portugal was initially accidental, according to most reports. Although Genoa was at peace with Portugal, his ship, bound to England, was attacked and destroyed just beyond the straits of Gibraltar, and Columbus was reportedly forced to come to shore clinging to an oar. The castaway was treated well by the Portuguese villagers he met on shore, and he proceeded to Lisbon, Portugal's capital, where he fell in with the city's small community of Genoese merchants and sailors. He remained based in Lisbon for the next decade, marrying a Portuguese woman and having a son, Diego.

Chapter 2: Columbus in Lisbon

Columbus's enterprise of sailing to the Indies emerged directly out of the cultural and economic environment he discovered in Lisbon. As John Noble Wilford has observed, "Ideas do not emerge in a vacuum. Even a man of his intuition, zeal, and self-assurance could not have conceived of such a scheme in a time much earlier or a place much different from Portugal in the late fifteenth century". Columbus's previous world had been that of the richly diverse but limited and fully charted Mediterranean; his world now was that of a country deeply engaged in exploration and expansion.

Since the fall of Constantinople, Portugal had begun to exploit its position at the edge of the Atlantic to set out to largely unmapped territories in search of new routes, new resources, and ultimately, a new path to the East that would circumvent the Ottoman blockade. But even prior to conceiving that goal, the Portuguese had been at the vanguard of oceanic exploration, and by the 1420s had already arrived at and established settlements on the Atlantic islands of Madeira and the Azores. The intellectual architect of Portuguese exploration was Prince Henry the Navigator, who was motivated by religious zeal to send expeditions down the Atlantic coast of Africa, initially hoping to check Muslim power on the continent and make contact with Prester John, a legendary Christian king in Africa (the legend was probably a garbled version of the Christian kingdom of Ethiopia). In the decades prior to Columbus's arrival in Lisbon, Portuguese expeditions had pushed farther and farther southward down the West African coast, opening up new trade in gold, ivory, and African slaves along the way. By the 1450s, the goal of circumnavigating Africa to reach Asia had been conceived.

Henry the Navigator

Furthermore, the Portuguese were being strongly encouraged by the Catholic Church. In the 1450s, the Pope issued papal bulls promising Portugal that at least among Catholic nations, Portugal would be given a trade monopoly in lands they discovered in Africa south of the Sahara. That was all the motivation the Portuguese needed: by then, the Portuguese had already sailed to Sierra Leone, on the western coast of Africa about half of the way down the continent. And in 1488, the Portuguese explorer Bartolomeu Dias became the first European to sail around the Cape of Good Hope, discovering much to his amazement that the Indian Ocean was connected to the Atlantic Ocean. One of the missions of Dias' expedition was to sail to India, which was a stated objective despite the fact the Portuguese did not realize they could sail around Africa to Asia. Dias did not reach India, but in 1497, Portugal's most famous explorer, Vasco da Gama sailed around Cape Good Hope, sailed north up the eastern coast of Africa and then sailed to Calicut, India, arriving in 1498.

Columbus would make his name by promoting a different route than that sought by the Portuguese, but the Portuguese explorers and traders had prepared the way for his ideas in several ways. First, the increasing confidence about long-distance sea travel, based in part on improved nautical technology and cartographical accuracy, made the notion of connecting distant regions by sea far more plausible than it had been even a hundred years earlier. For much of the Middle Ages, it was assumed that any routes connecting Europe and Asia would be land routes. Medieval cartography had always shown the possibility of sea routes, since they showed the three known continents of Europe, Asia, and Africa to be surrounded by a continuous body of water, but sea travel was regarded as far too dangerous and untested. The Portuguese explorations of the 15th century began to make this conviction look like an unfounded prejudice.

A second obstacle had been the belief, held since ancient times, that the Southern Hemisphere was an uninhabitable torrid zone where life could not thrive. Now the Portuguese had traveled much farther to the south than any Europeans before them and had found the climate pleasant, the vegetation abundant, and the ground rich in mineral deposits. These discoveries found confirmation in the rediscovered work of the ancient Greek geographer Ptolemy, who had painted a relatively pleasant picture of the tropical zones of Africa. In fact, the Portuguese would find so many inhabitants of Africa that when the Pope issued his papal bulls granting the Portuguese a trade monopoly in lands they discovered in south Africa, he gave the Portuguese the "right" to make "Saracens, pagans and any other unbelievers" slaves. Over the next 300 years, an estimated 10 million African slaves would be transported to the New World.

Columbus did not only imbibe the environment of Portugal's era of exploration – he also took part in it. Sometime around 1481, he participated in a voyage to the Guinea coast of West Africa, where he was impressed by the great abundance of gold that had been mined. During the same period, he supposedly heard multiple stories from Portuguese mariners suggesting that mysterious objects and even the bodies of unusual-looking men had been found washed ashore in several of Portugal's Atlantic settlements. Columbus also took advantage of his Atlantic expeditions to study winds and currents, the patterns of which apparently suggested to him the feasibility of westward travel out into the ocean.

Just as importantly, he became aware of the work of an Italian geographer based in Florence, Paolo Toscanelli, who on the basis both of recent Portuguese reports and of his prolonged studies of ancient cartography calculated that the shortest route to Asia lay across the Atlantic. Columbus apparently became aware of Toscanelli through the Florentine scientist's correspondence with a Portuguese acquaintance, Fernão Martins. Columbus himself wrote to Toscanelli in the early 1480s expressing enthusiasm for a westward route to the Indies and soliciting more details. Toscanelli was encouraging in his reply but died soon after writing it, leaving Columbus to continue his calculations on his own.

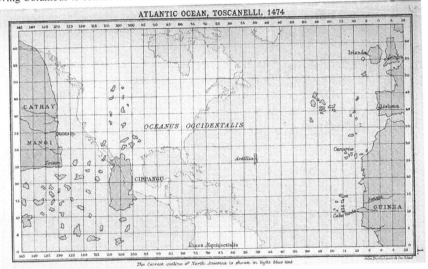

Toscanelli's map, calculating Asia's position across the Atlantic. Cathay was the word for China.

As Columbus's discussions with Toscanelli and Toscanelli's map make clear, the notion that Columbus "discovered that the earth was round" and had trouble finding backers for his enterprise because most of his contemporaries believed he would fall off the edge of the flat earth is one of the most blatant falsehoods of the many myths that have come to surround his biography over the centuries. The spherical shape of the earth had been assumed by educated Europeans for nearly two thousand years by the time Columbus arrived on the scene, and the groundwork for his enterprise had been laid by generations of geographers who worked with a relatively accurate picture not only of the earth's shape but of its dimensions.

The claim that the ignorant Spaniards and Portuguese of the 15th century believed in a flat earth seems to have been first introduced by the American writer Washington Irving, whose deliberately mythmaking 1828 biography made Columbus into a visionary advocate of empirical science in the face of medieval obscurantism. This characterization was at best highly exaggerated and at worst an outright falsification: Columbus certainly drew some of the evidence for the feasibility of his plans from the empirical discoveries of Portuguese explorers, but he also drew heavily on the traditional authorities, including the Bible, Aristotle, Ptolemy, Pliny and the more recent cosmography of Cardinal Pierre d'Ailly.

Columbus's true disagreement with many of his contemporaries had to do with a different question: the true circumference of the spherical earth, and the relative amount of its surface covered by land and by water. Different geographers and cosmographers had come to different conclusions, even though the Greek astronomer Eratosthenes had in fact calculated the earth's circumference quite accurately in the 3rd century B.C. In addition to the lack of empirical verification through circumnavigation, Eratosthenes's estimate had failed to become the consensus position because of confusion over the different systems and units of measurement used successively by Greeks, Romans, Arabs, and medieval Christians. Such confusion contributed to Columbus's calculation of a much shorter distance between the western tip of Europe and the eastern tip of Asia: when reading the estimates of medieval Arab cartographers, he took them to support the much smaller figure, when in fact they were simply working with a longer unit of measurement.

In any case Columbus developed his estimates from various sources, including Ptolemy, d'Ailly, Toscanelli, and certain obscure passages in the Bible, ultimately concluding that Asia lay at a distance of just under 4,000 kilometers. Here the Irving myth of Columbus the scientific pioneer becomes truly ironic: his estimate was as far off as could be, since the real distance was about 20,000 kilometers. As historian Edmund Morgan put it, "Columbus was not a scholarly man. Yet he studied these books, made hundreds of marginal notations in them and came out with ideas about the world that were characteristically simple and strong and sometimes wrong, the kind of ideas that the self-educated person gains from independent reading and clings to in defiance of what anyone else tries to tell him."

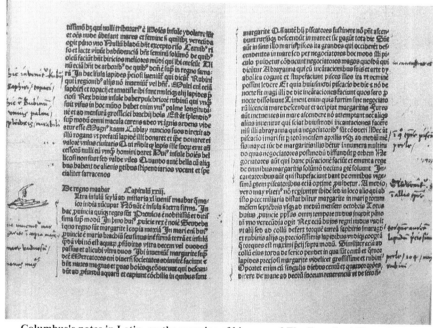

Columbus's notes in Latin, on the margins of his copy of *The Travels of Marco Polo*

The experts who ridiculed Columbus, far from being ignorant flat-earthers, were actually working from highly accurate measurements and had good reason to believe that Columbus's expedition would run out of water and supplies before reaching Asia. They only lacked one important piece of information: there was another land mass between Europe and Asia. This fact would both foil Columbus's initial goal of reaching Asia and ultimately place a different set of tasks before him.

Chapter 3: Columbus Searches for a Royal Sponsor

It was only natural that Columbus would first present his proposal to the Portuguese monarchy, which had sponsored so much exploration over the previous decades and had been reaping increasing rewards from their African trade routes. He did so for the first time in 1485, and after an initial rejection, returned with a second proposal in 1488, which met with an even more definitive rejection. In addition to the skepticism of King John II's official advisers, who correctly argued that Columbus's estimate of the distance to Asia was far too short, his plan was in competition with an alternative proposed route that would pass around the southern tip of Africa. This was clearly the safer option, and once the Portuguese navigator Bartholomew Diaz rounded the Cape of Good Hope and reached the Indian Ocean in 1488, Columbus's hopes for Portuguese support were dashed.

Since Portugal could already reach India, Columbus was forced to turn to rival powers for potential sponsorship. He made unsuccessful proposals to his home republic of Genoa and to Venice, both major seafaring powers whose Atlantic ambitions proved too modest, and to England, which also passed.

As it turned out, Columbus chose an auspicious moment to make his proposal to the so-called Catholic Monarchs of Spain, Ferdinand and Isabella. The two had married in 1769, uniting several previously separate kingdoms on the Iberian peninsula, most importantly the large kingdoms of Castile and Aragon. In the meantime, they had set out to reunite the peninsula under a fervently Catholic monarchy, which involved ridding their territories of non-Christian subjects. These efforts would come to a head in 1492 with the conquest of the southern kingdom of Granada from its Muslim rulers and the expulsion of all Jews who refused to accept baptism.

It was in this environment of territorial expansion, burgeoning military and political confidence, and evangelizing fervor that Columbus first brought his proposal to Spain. Partly due to his interest in the Bible and partly due to the religious nature of his audience, the proposal to sail west to the Indies that Columbus made to Ferdinand and Isabella was based on his interpretation of the Second Book of Esdras (2 Esdras 6:42), which Columbus interpreted as meaning the Earth was comprised of six parts of land to one of water. Although the monarchs, on advice from their official cosmographers, rejected the Genoese mariner's plan once again, they also provided him with a certain amount of encouragement, offering him a stipend if he chose to stay in Spain. Clearly, although they were uncertain about the plan, they did not wish Columbus to sell his ideas to a rival power such as Portugal, whose maritime advantage the Spanish crown was desperate to weaken.

Depiction of Ferdinand and Isabella

Two years later, in the wake of the successful Granada campaign, Columbus returned once more to Ferdinand and Isabella with his proposal and finally met with success. They accepted the terms he had proposed to all of the governments he had courted: three ships to undertake the voyage, the title of Admiral of the Ocean Sea, the title of Viceroy of any new lands he might claim for the Spanish crown, and the right to 10% of any revenue generated as a result of the trip. He and the Spanish monarchs signed their contract in the city of Córdoba, not far from the recently conquered Moorish capital of Granada. From there, he set out towards the small port of Palos de la Frontera, where he began to gather supplies and recruit crewmen.

Historians have long wondered why Columbus chose this small port, with limited resources, rather than the larger ports of Seville or Cádiz. One theory is that the resources in those two places were occupied with the thousands of Jewish refugees leaving Spain in the wake of the monarchs' edict of expulsion. In any case, Columbus hired the best ships he could find in Palos, contracting two caravels called the Niña and the Pinta from the Pinzón family and the third, which he called the Santa María, from cartographer Juan de la Cosa. Columbus referred to the Santa María as La Capitana ("The Flagship"), the Pinta was Spanish for "The Painted", and the Niña (Spanish for " Girl") was named after her owner, Juan Niño of Moguer. The real name of the Pinta is lost to history, while the Niña was actually named the Santa Clara.

The three ships set out on August 3, 1492.

Chapter 4: The First Voyage and its Impact

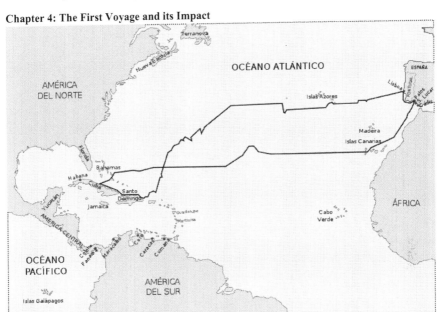

Columbus's First Voyage to and from the New World

Columbus would make history in October 1492, but the journey that landed him in the New World consisted of both crucial setbacks and a good deal of luck. The three ships would end up spending a total of just over two months on the Atlantic between continents, longer than what Columbus, with his optimistic measurement of the distance to Asia, had hoped for, but not so long as to cause mutiny or starvation.

The Castilian-sponsored expedition worked with several advantages. First, they were able to stop for supplies in early September in the conveniently placed Canary Islands, the one archipelago off the coast of West Africa that belonged to Castile rather than Portugal. Because the Portuguese crown had obtained papal guarantees of control over a large swath of the Atlantic seaboard, Columbus and his men had to be careful to avoid territories controlled by the rival power – not least because he did not wish to reveal his intentions to potential competitors. The Canaries provided a critical stopover for the expedition.

A second advantage, possibly but not certainly understood in advance by Columbus, were the "trade winds" blowing out of the East that prevailed as the ships sailed westward from the Canaries. The constant favorable wind allowed them to proceed at a brisk pace.

Finally, once they had proceeded some 300 leagues to the West of the Canary Islands, Columbus and his crew found themselves, to their surprise, in the midst of a highly pleasant, temperate climate, which seemed to improve as they proceeded.

Despite those advantages, the voyage is better known for its more harrowing circumstances. Just days into the journey from Spain, the rudder on the Pinta broke, disabling the ship and largely leading Columbus and his men to believe it had been sabotaged as a result of the fact the Pinta's owners and crew had not wanted the ship to be used in the journey. Columbus wrote of the incident in his journal (in which he refers to himself in the third person as Admiral), "It was believed that this happened by the contrivance of Gomez Rascon and Christopher Quintero, who were on board the caravel, because they disliked the voyage. The Admiral says he had found them in an unfavorable disposition before setting out. He was in much anxiety at not being able to afford any assistance in this case, but says that it somewhat quieted his apprehensions to know that Martin Alonzo Pinzon, Captain of the Pinta, was a man of courage and capacity."

After fixing the Pinta in the Canaries, the voyage ran into more trouble shortly after leaving from that point. On September 8, 1492, Columbus noticed his compass needle was no longer pointing due north, instead varying a half point to the Northwest and varying gradually further as the expedition continued. Columbus tried to keep this secret from the crew, which sparked even more anxiety when his pilots took notice. Columbus insisted that the needle was simply pointing to some invisible point on the Earth, and his reputation for knowing the stars allayed his crew's concerns. Unbeknownst to Columbus, his needle had started pointing to the Earth's magnetic north pole, something the Europeans knew nothing about.

The expedition was already getting antsy to spot land by mid-September, as evidenced by the journal entry Columbus made on September 14, 1492. "Friday, 14 September. Steered this day and night west twenty leagues; reckoned somewhat less. The crew of the Nina stated that they had seen a grajao, and a tropic bird, or water-wagtail, which birds never go farther than twenty-five leagues from the land."

Two days later, Columbus already noted in his journal that he had taken up the practice of recording that the ships had sailed less distance than they actually had. He also continued to find evidence of land even as land sightings evaded his crew. "Sunday, 16 September. Sailed day and night, west thirty-nine leagues, and reckoned only thirty-six. Some clouds arose and it drizzled. The Admiral here says that from this time they experienced very pleasant weather, and that the mornings were most delightful, wanting nothing but the melody of the nightingales. He compares the weather to that of Andalusia in April. Here they began to meet with large patches of weeds very green, and which appeared to have been recently washed away from the land; on which account they all judged themselves to be near some island, though not a continent, according to the opinion of the Admiral, who says, 'the continent we shall find further ahead.'"

Columbus noted the uneasiness of his crew on September 23. "Sunday, 23 September. Sailed northwest and northwest by north and at times west nearly twenty-two leagues. Saw a turtle dove, a pelican, a river bird, and other white fowl;--weeds in abundance with crabs among them. The sea being smooth and tranquil, the sailors murmured, saying that they had got into smooth water, where it would never blow to carry them back to Spain; but afterwards the sea rose without wind, which astonished them. The Admiral says on this occasion 'the rising of the sea was very favorable to me, as it happened formerly to Moses when he led the Jews from Egypt.'"

One of the first major false sightings of land took place on September 25, as recounted by Columbus. "At sunset Martin Alonzo called out with great joy from his vessel that he saw land, and demanded of the Admiral a reward for his intelligence. The Admiral says, when he heard him declare this, he fell on his knees and returned thanks to God, and Martin Alonzo with his crew repeated Gloria in excelsis Deo, as did the crew of the Admiral. Those on board the Nina ascended the rigging, and all declared they saw land. The Admiral also thought it was land, and about twenty-five leagues distant. They remained all night repeating these affirmations, and the Admiral ordered their course to be shifted from west to southwest where the land appeared to lie. They sailed that day four leagues and a half west and in the night seventeen leagues southwest, in all twenty-one and a half: told the crew thirteen leagues, making it a point to keep them from knowing how far they had sailed; in this manner two reckonings were kept, the shorter one falsified, and the other being the true account. The sea was very smooth and many of the sailors went in it to bathe, saw many dories and other fish."

By October 10, Columbus's crew was on the verge of losing all hope. "Wednesday, 10 October. Steered west-southwest and sailed at times ten miles an hour, at others twelve, and at others, seven; day and night made fifty-nine leagues' progress; reckoned to the crew but forty-four. Here the men lost all patience, and complained of the length of the voyage, but the Admiral encouraged them in the best manner he could, representing the profits they were about to acquire, and adding that it was to no purpose to complain, having come so far, they had nothing to do but continue on to the Indies, till with the help of our Lord, they should arrive there."

Thankfully for Columbus, the expedition actually sighted land the following night, on October 11, 1492. Ironically, after all the false reports about sighting land, Columbus was initially skeptical when the crew actually did see land, writing on October 11, "The crew of the Pinta saw a cane and a log; they also picked up a stick which appeared to have been carved with an iron tool, a piece of cane, a plant which grows on land, and a board. The crew of the Nina saw other signs of land, and a stalk loaded with rose berries. These signs encouraged them, and they all grew cheerful. Sailed this day till sunset, twenty-seven leagues. After sunset steered their original course west and sailed twelve miles an hour till two hours after midnight, going ninety miles, which are twenty-two leagues and a half; and as the Pinta was the swiftest sailer, and kept ahead of the Admiral, she discovered land and made the signals which had been ordered. The land was first seen by a sailor called Rodrigo de Triana, although the Admiral at ten o'clock that evening standing on the quarter-deck saw a light, but so small a body that he could not affirm it to be land."

Scholars have long attempted to determine which of the many tiny islands that now make up the Bahamas and Turks and Caicos Islands it might have been, but the mystery remains. It is known from Columbus's and other accounts that the inhabitants of the island called it Guanahaní; Columbus, upon setting foot there and claiming it for the Castilian crown, called it San Salvador (Holy Savior). While the excitement of landfall was obviously enormous, it should be recalled that Columbus was likely very puzzled by what he encountered: naked or semi-naked people with no apparent material wealth beyond the odd trinket or piece of jewelry, and with no permanent abodes of a recognizable European type. He had set out, after all, in search of what was then the wealthiest and most economically advanced region of the world: Asia, which he believed to be ruled by the fabulously opulent Great Khan described by Marco Polo. Columbus's earlier communiqués, then, are somewhat unreliable in that they comprise an attempt to make the best of unexpected circumstances. Since he has found none of the great sources of wealth he sought, he instead celebrates the gentleness, simplicity, and innocence of the people he has discovered, as well as the tropical abundance of the land.

According to Columbus's journal, these were his exact words upon coming into contact with the indigenous natives:

"As I saw that they were very friendly to us, and perceived that they could be much more easily converted to our holy faith by gentle means than by force, I presented them with some red caps, and strings of beads to wear upon the neck, and many other trifles of small value, wherewith they were much delighted, and became wonderfully attached to us. Afterwards they came swimming to the boats, bringing parrots, balls of cotton thread, javelins, and many other things which they exchanged for articles we gave them, such as glass beads, and hawk's bells; which trade was carried on with the utmost good will. But they seemed on the whole to me, to be a very poor people. They all go completely naked, even the women, though I saw but one girl. All whom I saw were young, not above thirty years of age, well made, with fine shapes and faces; their hair short, and coarse like that of a horse's tail, combed toward the forehead, except a small portion which they suffer to hang down behind, and never cut. Some paint themselves with black, which makes them appear like those of the Canaries, neither black nor white; others with white, others with red, and others with such colors as they can find. Some paint the face, and some the whole body; others only the eyes, and others the nose. Weapons they have none, nor are acquainted with them, for I showed them swords which they grasped by the blades, and cut themselves through ignorance. They have no iron, their javelins being without it, and nothing more than sticks, though some have fish-bones or other things at the ends. They are all of a good size and stature, and handsomely formed. I saw some with scars of wounds upon their bodies, and demanded by signs the of them; they answered me in the same way, that there came people from the other islands in the neighborhood who endeavored to make prisoners of them, and they defended themselves. I thought then, and still believe, that these were from the continent."

Columbus's log and his early letter to his financier Luis de Santángel, which are the earliest accounts of the "discovery," project a politically expedient confidence and optimism since he did not wish to lose his contract with Ferdinand and Isabella, but Columbus was likely very confused by what he found. The people and their way of life clashed with what he expected, and the disposition of the many small islands he found was difficult to reconcile with the maps of the East Asian coast he had so avidly studied. His most important goal was to reach *terra firma*, since it was there that he would find the great trading empires whose wealth he wished to tap into. Thus, the early accounts contain a number of strategies of interpretation that attempt to fit what he has found into his preconceived framework. First of all, he attempted to map the territories he found in the Caribbean, however improbably, onto Asian geography as he understood it. The northern islands of the Bahamas, he imagines, may be part of the island empire of Cipango (Japan); the long coast of Cuba, where he arrived next by heading to the Southwest, must be part of China. Second, in his repeated emphasis on the gentleness and peacefulness of the natives, he is also insisting on their status as "natural slaves," an intellectual category used in the ancient world to justify slavery. More specifically, he concluded, they must be among the peoples from whom the Great Khan drew his many slaves; at the same time, he set the stage for the slavery-based colonization that would soon overtake the Caribbean islands and, within a few decades, wipe out their entire indigenous population. In fact, Columbus began this trend by essentially kidnapping six Guanahaní natives, in his words, "so that they will learn to speak," i.e. become interpreters for the expedition.

On San Salvador and several subsequent small islands, Columbus proceeded in the same way: he claimed the territory for Spain, announcing to the uncomprehending inhabitants that they were now subjects of the King and Queen, engaged in small-scale barter with the natives, giving them what were for them unusual glass beads and bells in exchange for parrots, javelins, and other local objects, and looking around for anything that seemed to be of real value, according to his standards. Here he was soon successful, or so he thought, because some of the "Indians," as he called them (in an error whose effects on nomenclature remain to this day) were wearing small pieces of gold as nose rings and earrings. This was, to Columbus's mind, his first indication of the famed wealth of the East: gold was so abundant that even these poor and marginal peoples possessed some.

No sooner did he catch sight of gold than he began asking after its origin. His inquiries propelled him toward the large island of Cuba, which he was desperate to interpret as part of the mainland coast. He called it La Juana, and after a brief stop, proceeded to the island he would call La Española (anglicized to Hispaniola). It was here that the Santa María ran aground on a shallow coral reef and was damaged, leading to the establishment of the first permanent Spanish settlement on Christmas Day, 1492, which was duly named La Navidad. The marooned men were treated generously by the local Taino Indians, and it seemed as safe a place as any to lay a settlement; furthermore, there were reports that they were close to the enormous gold deposits they were looking for. It was perhaps because of this that the men were eager to stay behind in La Navidad rather than proceed onward.

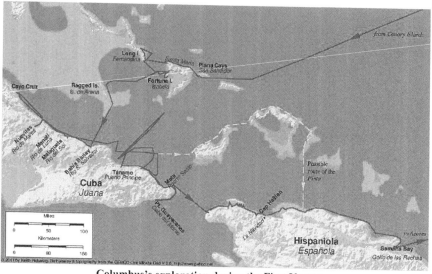

Columbus's exploration during the First Voyage

For reasons that are not entirely clear, Columbus decided at this point to proceed with great haste back to Spain, as he announced in his log on January 8, 1493. Since he believed that he had ultimately come close to a source of great wealth, he may have wished to return with reinforcements in the instance of any hostilities. After all, Columbus believed the great armies of the Khan could have been nearby. Furthermore, Columbus may have sought to reassure the Spanish Crown of his success and guarantee his share of the wealth that he now felt confident about extracting from the lands he had encountered.

Whatever the explanation of his choice to end his first voyage, it marked a turning point in his career. He had so far spent over five months at sea and three months exploring with no major setbacks, no mutinies and no hostile encounters with the natives. All of this was about to change, and the early idyll of friendly encounters with generous "Indians" would come to an end abruptly on January 13, on the eastern end of La Española, in what is now the Dominican Republic. The Spaniards, as was their habit, had come ashore to barter with a group of natives, but the barter did not go as planned, and a miscommunication led to an outbreak of hostilities in which two natives were injured. Subsequently, Columbus theorized that there were two in fact two groups of natives: the peaceful Tainos with whom he had met previously, and the hostile and violent Caribs, whom he claimed other natives had told him were man-eaters or "cannibals" (the term, coined in Columbus's diary, comes from the same uncertain indigenous lexeme as "Caribbean").

In La Navidad, the first European settlement in the Americas since Leif Ericsson's Norse colony in Newfoundland, things would go even worse. When Columbus returned on his second voyage in November, 1493, he found the village a charred ruin. The men, presumably as a result of their rapacious desire for gold and probable abuse of local women, eventually earned the hostility of nearby tribes, who promptly exterminated them. The consensual and peaceful colonization that Columbus had promised to undertake had been little more than a brief illusion.

By the time Columbus started setting east from the New World, he had explored San Salvador in the Bahamas (which he thought it was Japan, Cuba (which he thought was China), and Hispaniola, the source of gold. Due to the prevailing winds, Columbus took the Niña and the Pinta back to Spain by a completely different route, this time passing through the Portuguese-controlled Azores islands in the mid-Atlantic. Subsequently, storms at sea obliged him to dock in Lisbon before proceeding to Seville, and then on to Toledo and Barcelona, where he received a hero's welcome from a populace that had already received word of his supposed arrival in Asia. The Catholic Monarchs were currently holding court in Spain's great Mediterranean port of Barcelona, where a copy of Columbus's rhapsodic letter to Santángel had already been reproduced on a mechanical printing press (recently invented by Gutenberg) and circulated among the literate populace. Columbus also bore gifts of tobacco, pineapple, and a turkey, and he assured his hosts that gold as well as valuable spices would be forthcoming on his next expedition. They were evidently impressed, and fêted the "admiral and viceroy" at court for about five weeks.

In the meantime, Columbus and his sponsors were already scheming; they were concerned, particularly after his initial landfall in Portugal, that King John II might send his well-prepared fleets in pursuit of the lands Columbus had reached. In order to forestall further conflict with the rival Iberian kingdom, they sent an official request to the Pope for an official title to the new lands (as God's right-hand man, the Pope was understood to have jurisdiction over the entire globe). The result was a decree granting Spain sovereignty over the lands Columbus had reached and all territories to the West, while Portugal would obtain control over any territories to the East. This arrangement would ultimately result in the division of South America between the Spanish-speaking countries stretching from Argentina up the west coast of the continent to Venezuela and Portuguese-speaking Brazil occupying the eastern half of the land mass.

Chapter 5: The Second Voyage and the Beginnings of Colonization

On the heels of his apparent success and the approval of the Spanish crown, Columbus managed to assemble a much larger fleet for his second trip across the Atlantic, which began on September 24, 1492. His expeditionary force now consisted of 17 ships, including the Niña but neither of the other two vessels from the previous voyage. It is clear from the number of men and quantity of supplies carried over that Columbus now intended to establish more permanent settlements and pave the way for the establishment of full-scale colonies. He also brought with him a contingent of friars, who would be entrusted with the evangelization of the natives.

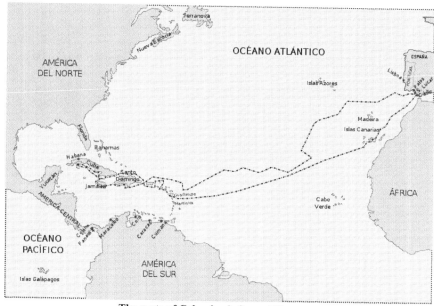

The route of Columbus's Second Voyage

Perhaps because he believed that he would reach the mainland (China) more directly, Columbus now tacked further to the south than he had on the first crossing. Instead, he found the long series of small islands that make up the Lesser Antilles. There, he found more of what he had found in the Bahamas: small-scale societies possessing no obvious material wealth. Having encountered and claimed several of these small islands for Spain, he proceeded back toward the Greater Antilles, the large islands he had repeatedly mistaken for the Asian coast.

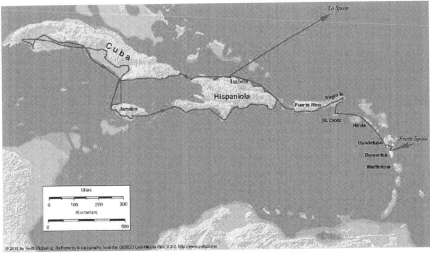

Columbus's exploration during his Second Voyage

One of the peculiarities of the second voyage is that Columbus succeeded in charting out most of what is now known as the Caribbean, but was unaware that this was what he was doing, so determined was he to find his way to the wealthy kingdoms of the East and so adept was he at fitting the geography he encountered into his schema. For instance, after he had proceeded along the southern coasts of the same islands whose northern coasts he explored on the previous trip, he still refused to consider that Cuba was an island. Instead, he assumed it was a peninsula jutting off the coast of Asia.

After skirting along the Lesser Antilles, Columbus and his crew passed first along the coast of what is now Puerto Rico, where they had another brief outbreak of hostilities with a group of natives. This skirmish set the far more violent tone for the rest of the trip. He soon proceeded to Hispaniola, where he found the ruins of La Navidad and began to investigate the causes of the falling out with the natives, deciding to blame a group of Tainos distinct from the band he had initially established an agreement with when the settlement was laid. He also took an expedition into the interior of the island, where he succeeded in finding gold deposits and established a fortress.

The two near-simultaneous discoveries – the ruined village of La Navidad and the definite presence of gold on Hispaniola – had nefarious consequences that would exercise a decisive impact on the nature of Spanish colonization and on the later history of the territories Columbus had encountered. The Spaniards established a new settlement, named La Isabela after the queen, but the conditions were harsh, and the men, disturbed by the evidence of massacre at La Navidad and by the lack of immediate enrichment, were restless and hostile to Columbus's authority. In the meantime, Columbus became increasingly concerned about further attacks from the local natives. In order to forestall what he perceived might be an impending disaster, he went on the offense, capturing well over 1,000 supposedly hostile Indians to sell into slavery. He sent a letter to the queen, whose piety made her morally uncomfortable with slavery, arguing that these particular Indians were cannibals prone to violence, and that they could only be reformed through forced servitude. She was unmoved by the argument, but Columbus proceeded with the plan against her orders anyway. Just as brutally, he now exacted a tribute from the remaining Indians of the island, demanding that they bring a certain quota of gold or cotton to the Spanish authorities every three months. The demands were impossible to fulfill given the modest deposits available, and the results on Spanish-Taino relations, and on Taino demography, would be disastrous.

Columbus's decision to resort to enslavement and a tribute system resulted in part from his own desperate circumstances. He had promised great things when last in Spain, and the many financiers who had invested in the expedition along with the king and queen would need to see a return on investment. Columbus had banked everything on success in his second voyage, and if he came up short, his credit and his contract with the crown would likely be ruined, so he resorted to the most efficient ways to extract wealth, placate his men and subdue the increasingly hostile natives.

Unfortunately, the entire enterprise was impossible, because the islands he had conquered simply did not have adequate resources to satisfy the demands his promises had created. The result of his tribute system was not a flood of wealth but the exhaustion of both the small gold deposits and the good will of the Tainos, who now understandably entered into open conflict with the invaders. Meanwhile, the Spanish settlers, who had come on the voyage expecting great and immediate material gain, were angry and nearly as hostile to the ostensible "viceroy" as the natives whose land he had appropriated. In order to escape the chaos that had consumed La Isabela, Columbus set out on another maritime expedition exploring the island of Jamaica and left his brother Diego in charge. Diego proved an even less popular leader, and the rage of the Spaniards continued to spill out onto the local natives, who fell victim to several massacres.

By 1496, Columbus became aware that negative reports about his leadership in Hispaniola had reached the Spanish king and queen. Partly in order to engage in damage control, and partly to solicit resources for a further expedition, he returned to Spain in March of that year. His brothers Diego and Bartholomew remained in charge, and he left instructions to build another town, since the location of La Isabela had proved unsustainable. The new settlement would be Santo Domingo, the only one of Columbus's settlements on Hispaniola to survive, but Bartholomew and Diego would prove incompetent leaders, and their failures would set the stage for the disasters of Columbus's third voyage.

For the moment, however, Columbus managed to persuade the monarchy to sponsor his next expedition. They had invested a great deal of effort in lobbying the Pope for control over the lands he found, and they were not willing to take a loss on the sum they had put into funding Columbus and in the process potentially lose control of the conquered territories.

Chapter 6: The Third and Fourth Voyages - Disaster and Disgrace

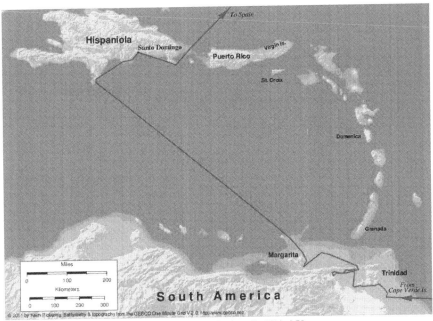

Columbus's exploration during the Third Voyage

Columbus's third expedition, which began in May of 1498, set out with fewer than half the number of ships he had taken five years earlier. Three of the six ships that set out for the Indies would proceed directly to Hispaniola, carrying provisions for the settlers, while Columbus took the other three ships on an expedition further south in the hope of finally reaching the Asian mainland. The ships passed through the southernmost Atlantic islands then colonized, the Portuguese-controlled Cape Verde islands, and then headed even further to the south, coming closer to the equator than he ever had before.

This time Columbus did reach terra firma, but not the terra firma he was expecting. He arrived in the Gulf of Paria in what is now Venezuela, where the vast Orinoco River, with its source in the Amazon, pours into the sea. From the abundance of fresh water he discovered, Columbus knew that what he had found could only be another continent – but certainly not the eastern coast of Asia, which he knew possessed no rivers spilling northward into the ocean. The resulting confusion gave birth to Columbus's most extravagant literary fantasy: in a letter back to Spain, he claimed that the new continent he had discovered was the Earthly Paradise. Conveniently, legend had it that great deposits of gold lay in the vicinity of this mythical place, which allowed him to maintain an optimistic tone.

Whatever degree of confidence the discovery of an indisputable mainland had produced in Columbus, it was severely counteracted in the next stage of his trip. He returned to Hispaniola in order to check on the settlement he had left in the care of his two brothers, only to find conditions even more catastrophic than when he had left. Bartholomew and Diego had managed to gain the undying enmity of both the Spanish colonists and of the Tainos, and both groups were in open and violent mutiny against their rule, while at the same time perpetrating increasingly merciless war against each other. Columbus retaliated against some of the most recalcitrant Spaniards, using his authority to prosecute them and send them to the gallows, but his harsh measures lost him the sympathy of even those in the colony who remained loyal, and several of them managed to convey a covert message to the crown demanding that it send an emissary to investigate the ineffectual rule of the Columbus brothers and restore order.

The result was catastrophic as far as Columbus's personal fortunes were concerned. The Spanish judge who arrived, Francisco de Bobadilla, issued a harsh repudiation of the Columbuses, stripped Christopher of his titles, and sent him back to Spain in shackles in October 1500. It was on his undoubtedly miserable voyage back across the Atlantic that Columbus composed the letter claiming that he had come close to the Earthly Paradise as well as to the great mines of King Solomon.

On one level, this outlandish claim looks to have been a clever strategy to persuade the king and queen that he was close to further and even more significant discoveries, in the hope that they would be merciful with him. It was effective, in so far as Columbus was released from prison and given the right to argue his case at court. On the other hand, the Book of Prophecies that Columbus began compiling in this period suggests that he did in fact believe that his was a divinely appointed mission that would bring the heathen world into Christendom and prepare the way for Christ's second coming. His feverish recourse to biblical citations may have reflected his true understanding of his appointed role.

Whatever, the case, he succeeded in regaining his admiralty but not his position as viceroy, and the crown permitted him to undertake a fourth (and ultimately final) voyage. It is unclear whether they acted out of pity, out of deep conviction, or out of fear that he might sell his nautical services and territorial knowledge to a rival like Genoa or Portugal. In any case, he was equipped with a relatively small fleet of four vessels. The newly appointed governor of Hispaniola, to which Columbus was now forbidden to return, set out around the same time with a fleet of thirty.

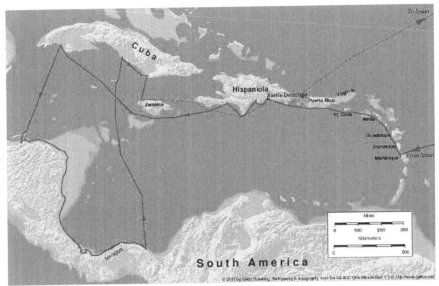

Columbus's exploration during his Fourth Voyage

Columbus's fourth journey was the most disastrous yet, and ended in career-destroying humiliation. He set out from Cádiz on May 9, 1502 and arrived in Hispaniola less than two months later, where he was promptly denied the right to dock his ships. He proceeded west and then south across the Caribbean, aiming to approach the continent he had skirted on his previous voyage from a different angle. He was successful in this endeavor, and by the end of July he and his crew had reached the coast of what is now Honduras, a terra firma continuous with the distant Venezuelan coast he had explored years back.

Columbus and his ships next proceeded southeast down the Central American coast, on the lookout for evidence of material wealth or a strait leading to India. Interestingly, had they proceeded inland in certain spots or made their way north toward the Yucatán, they would have encountered remnants of the great Mayan civilization, which had now been in decline for some time. It would, at least, have corresponded more to Columbus's presuppositions about the wealthy, urban civilizations of the East. Instead, they met more small-scale groups, a number of which showed a marked hostility to the newcomers. Off the coast of what is now Panama, they began to discover promising quantities of gold, and Columbus decreed that a settlement would be founded there. But it was not to be. Persistent native attacks ultimately drove the would-be colonists back in the direction they had come from, and on the attempted return to Hispaniola, they shipwrecked off the coast of Jamaica. There, the "Admiral of the Ocean Sea," again a castaway as he had been in Portugal at the beginning of his career, sent a desperate letter to Spain requesting reinforcements to assist in the colonization effort in Panama. He received no reply.

Chapter 7: Columbus's Final Years

Despised as he was by the authorities in Hispaniola, the marooned Columbus had to wait nearly a year to be rescued and sent back to Spain, where he arrived near the end of 1504. At this point, both his health and his reputation were at a low point, and his situation was not helped by the death of his main sponsor, Queen Isabella, soon after his arrival.

With his chances at court as well as his own stamina so diminished, he settled in the port of Seville and used his remaining fortune to begin a litigation for the restoration of his titles and rights. He continued to insist, in his final years of life, that he had reached the far perimeter of the Indies, despite the lack of obvious correspondence between the lands he had discovered and the relatively accurate maps of Asia known to Europeans at the time, not to mention the lack of contact with any of the known peoples or products of the East. Confident of his accomplishments, he visited the court in several locations and attempted to gain a final audience, but to no avail. He went to his grave with his legacy and reputation highly uncertain.

When Columbus died on May 20, 1506, his sons were forced to take up his case in order to establish what they regarded as their rightful inheritance. As part of this effort, his son Hernando, who had accompanied him on his final journey, began to compose the first biography of his father, which recapitulated Christopher's saintly self-image in attempt to redeem him in the eyes of the authorities and the public. Hernando's criticisms of the monarchy, however, made it difficult to publish, and the biography was still not in print by the time of his own death in 1539.

Meanwhile, the Dominican priest Bartolomé de las Casas, who edited and commented Columbus's log from his first voyage in preparation for the composition of his own *History of the Indies*, took a very different angle on the great admiral's life. A harsh critic of the cruelty of the Spaniards to the Indians, Las Casas shared Columbus's own conviction that his mission was divinely inspired, but he believed that the brutality and enslavement first unleashed by Columbus and perpetuated in more extreme forms by his successors had utterly derailed the true goal of the discovery: the evangelization of the natives, which he believed should have proceeded peacefully and consensually.

Las Casas waged an all-out battle against Spain's colonial enterprise and gained a sympathetic hearing at court, but the juggernaut of conquest had been unleashed, and the Spanish authorities proved either unwilling or unable to restrain most of the brutality unleashed by the conquistadors against the original inhabitants of the lands.

Chapter 8: Magellan's Trips to the Indies

Today Ferdinand Magellan is remembered as the first man to circumnavigate the globe, an ironic legacy given that he died half a world away from completing that journey. But one of the things most overlooked is the fact that he was conducting his historic voyage at the same time as some of his most famous contemporaries.

Unlike Christopher Columbus, who was from an Italian mercantile background, and unlike Cortés, who came from an impoverished family of noble lineage in the remote province of Extremadura, Ferdinand Magellan was born into the heart of the Portuguese aristocracy. His father, Rui de Magalhães, was an official in the city of Aveiro, and the family of his mother, Alda de Mesquita, was well connected at court. As a result of this prestigious background, when his parents died while he was still a young boy, 10 year old Ferdinand became a page of Queen Leonor, whose husband King John II reigned from 1481-1495 and was then succeeded by her brother, King Manuel I. While such figures as Cortés and Pizarro were clearly motivated in part or entirely by the desire to enrich themselves and gain an improved social position through their foreign conquests, Magellan's motivations must have been quite different, as he could presumably have led a comfortable life of privilege in Portugal given his early background and connections. But given the cultural milieu of 15th century Portugal, it is not at all surprising that he chose the path he did.

Just a year before Columbus's death, and just a year after Cortes headed to the New World, Magellan's early career unfolded in the newly established Portuguese Indies, where he first sailed around 1505 under the command of Francisco de Almeida, whom the Portuguese crown had appointed Viceroy of India. The available records do not make clear where he spent his first few years in the new territories of the Indian Ocean, but in addition to India, he is likely to have visited Malaysia and the African territory of Mozambique. Unlike in the Caribbean, where Columbus and his successors found for the most part small-scale societies with disappointingly low levels of trade and meager supplies of desirable commodities, Magellan and the other early Portuguese denizens of the Indian Ocean found themselves amidst a far more sophisticated network of commerce than any in Europe of the time. Arab, Indian, and Chinese merchants could be found around the entire perimeter of the Indian Ocean, and in cities of Malaysia dozens of African, Middle Eastern, and Asian languages could be heard. Furthermore, it was essentially a peaceful region, bound together by mutual economic interest and a religious unity fostered by centuries of Islamic dominance. While the "Indies" that Columbus reached proved a disappointment (at least initially), the Indian Ocean region was as wealthy and abundant in precious commodities as the Portuguese had hoped, and they soon took decisive measures to assure their control there.

In February 1509, the Portuguese won a crucial victory against the Ottoman Turks and their allied forces (including, curiously, the Italian Republic of Venice) at Diu in southwestern India. Within just over ten years of Vasco da Gama's expedition, the Portuguese had dealt a definitive blow to Muslim hegemony in the Indian Ocean. Although it was less a territorial conquest than an establishment of naval control over trade routes, it was as remarkable and unlikely a turn of events as Cortés's and Pizarro's overthrow of the great empires of the Americas. Magellan was present for the Battle of Diu, and also took part the following year in the conquest of the Indian city of Goa, which would remain a Portuguese colony until the 20th century. Having essentially extinguished Muslim power along the coasts of the African and Asian mainlands, the Portuguese turned their attention to the Malaysian city of Malacca. Malacca was an international port and trade center that stood on the Strait of Malacca, which separated the Asian continent from the archipelagos of present-day Malaysia and Indonesia. This meant control over Malacca would provide a gateway to the immense wealth of the Spice Islands to the South. A Portuguese force under Alonso de Alburquerque besieged Malacca for six weeks in 1511, and Magellan was among the conquerors who entered the city when it fell.

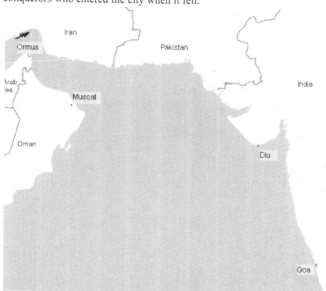

Points of Portuguese control in the Indian Ocean during the early 16th century

Toward the end of 1511, Magellan may or may not have participated in a trade and reconnaissance expedition to the Spice Islands, but regardless of whether or not he actually went, he could have gleaned a great deal of intelligence about them in his new location. In the meantime, he was honored with promotion and awarded with a sizable share of the expedition's rich plunder. He also took a Malay man captive as a slave and baptized him with the Christian name Enrique. Enrique accompanied Magellan back to Portugal in 1512, and would return to his place of origin as a translator for Magellan's westward voyage back to the Indian Ocean some years later. In this sense, it was Enrique who may have been the first person to truly circumnavigate the globe, since it's presumed he would make it back to Malaysia during Magellan's voyage. In reality, it is uncertain what became of Enrique after Magellan's death, as his name drops from reliable historical records at this point. Whatever his ultimate fate, Enrique stands with Cortés's translator and consort Doña Marina and Pizarro's captive Felipillo as a remarkable non-European (and involuntary) participant in the Age of Exploration whose life has generally been overshadowed by that of his European captor.

Magellan returned to Portugal in 1513, having spent eight years in the Indies. It is not clear what motivated his return to his home country, but one theory is that he was hoping to find a way of gaining a greater fortune and more prestigious position in the new Portuguese colonies by utilizing his royal connections in Lisbon.

In the meantime, Magellan remained in contact with his friend (and possibly cousin) Francisco Serrão, with whom he had sailed in 1505 and who remained in Malucca. Serrão traveled around the Spice Islands on several occasions and his letters provided his friend with useful intelligence on the topography and politics of the region, which he would subsequently put to use when planning his return to the East. Had his career ended when he sailed back to Lisbon in 1513, Magellan's name would not be remembered. He would be only one of thousands who took part in the remarkably rapid and successful Portuguese expansion into the Indian Ocean, a process that, interestingly enough, produced no names that have gone down in history in the manner of Columbus, Cortés, Pizarro, Balboa, de Soto, or Coronado. Although the Portuguese had sacked a number of cities and slaughtered their inhabitants much like the Spaniards were doing in the New World, their fundamental approach differed in that they were far more concerned with controlling trade than with conquering vast territories. As it turned out, Magellan would end up making a name for himself by going into the service of Spain, Portugal's greatest imperial rival of the era.

Even after its successes in Asia, Portugal was still deeply involved militarily and commercially in the more proximate African continent, both because of ongoing conflicts with pirates from North Africa, because of religious enmity with Islam, and because of its involvement in the slave trade and other enterprises. Soon after his arrival back in Portugal, Magellan joined an expedition led by the Duke of Braganza against Azamor, a city in Morocco that had been conquered by the Portuguese in 1486. After the conquest, the inhabitants of Azamor were obliged to pay an annual tribute to the crown of Portugal, but in 1513 local ruler Moulay Zayam refused to pay the tribute and revolted against the Portuguese, gathering a sizable army to throw the invaders out. The king decided to respond with deadly force against this act of insubordination and sent a large expeditionary army of some 15,000 troops to put down the Moroccan rebels. There is some evidence to suggest that this strong resolve was motivated more by a desire not to show weakness than by genuine advantage; although the Portuguese would prove victorious, the victory would be somewhat Pyrrhic. They would ultimately be forced to abandon Azamor because the cost of maintaining their control there exceeded the revenues brought in by tribute payments and trade.

Magellan, by now an experienced veteran of several major sieges and battles, joined the Portuguese fleet that sailed down to Azamor, but it turned out to be one of the more ill-fated decisions of his career. During the hostilities there, he lost his horse and suffered a leg wound that left him with a pronounced limp for the rest of his life.

Even after the final victory over Zayam and his forces had been won, things continued not to go nearly as well for Magellan as they had in the East. As a participant in the successful conquest, he was given a share of the spoils of war, but he was then accused by superior officers of engaging in illegal trade with the Moroccans for selling some of the items he had been awarded back to inhabitants of Azamor at a profit. Although he was ultimately cleared of this accusation, it appears to have become something of a stain on his record, and the word of his supposed wrongdoing probably reached the Portuguese court relatively quickly. A continued aura of suspicion surrounding him seems to have worsened his standing with King Manuel, whose sister he had served as a page early in his life. When he returned to Lisbon in November 1415 and requested an increase in his pension as a reward for his service in Morocco, he was refused. Likewise, his requests to participate in various Portuguese expeditions were also refused. It was apparent the king and his advisors no longer trusted him.

King Manuel I of Portugal

It was around this period that Magellan began to hatch a plan to sail to the Spice Islands by sailing west across the Atlantic. The geography of the Americas was still only dimly understood at this point, but Magellan believed like Columbus before him that this would surely be the most efficient route to Asia. Unaware that Columbus had discovered a new continent, unaware of the scope of the Pacific Ocean, and unaware of how far south the South American continent stretched, Magellan imagined it would save the trouble of sailing all the way around the southern tip of Africa to reach the Indian Ocean. With these arguments, he petitioned the king to lead an expedition, also noting that the Spanish, now well-established in the islands to the East of the Indian Ocean (the Americas), might reach the Spice Islands from that direction and claim jurisdiction over them by invoking the Treaty of Tordesillas. Magellan was unsuccessful in his several petitions to the king, who seems to have permanently retracted his trust in him, and finally, in 1516, he requested and was given leave to present his petition to other rulers.

With that, he crossed the border into Spain. Here his path again closely follows that of Columbus, who had also repeatedly presented his plan for a westward journey to the Indies to the

Portuguese crown. Magellan first went to Seville in 1517, where he met with other Portuguese mariners and conferred with the Portuguese cosmographer Rui Faleiro. Based on Faleiro's geographical knowledge and the intelligence Magellan had gleaned from his time in the Indies and the letters of Serrão, they hatched a plan that must have seemed irresistible to the Spanish crown. Not only would a westward journey to the Spice Islands offer precisely what Columbus had promised (but not delivered) to Ferdinand and Isabella in the 1490s, it would avoid overt conflict with the Portuguese, who had already staked out the eastward route to the Indian Ocean. Furthermore, based on Faleiro's cartography and calculations, Magellan and Faleiro believed that their western location made the Spice Islands part of the territory granted to Spain as part of the Treaty of Tordesillas.

Magellan's decision to undercut the territorial gains of the country he had been born in and served has made him a less than heroic figure for Portuguese historians, who have branded him a traitor. Indeed, it seems quite likely that Magellan was trying to settle scores with the Portuguese crown, at least to some extent. However, he had also first proposed his expedition to Portugal's King Manuel, and upon being rebuffed he simply did what other explorers of his era, including Columbus, John Cabot, and Amerigo Vespucci, had also done: sought sponsorship for his enterprise, in whatever form it took, and whoever it came from.

Magellan's petition at the Spanish court in Valladolid met with more immediate success than Columbus's had 30 years before. He was, of course, proceeding from more solid information than his Genoese predecessor, having already spent eight years in the destination region himself, and his maps and proposed route were far less controversial. King Charles I, the grandson of Ferdinand and Isabella who would later become the Holy Roman Emperor and the most powerful ruler in Europe, did not hesitate long in granting Magellan and Faleiro most of their requests. They were appointed joint captains of the proposed expedition, made knights of the prestigious Order of Santiago, and granted a 10-year monopoly on all trade on their route and 5% of all profits from the route and the governorship of an island each. The crown would also cover the up-front costs of obtaining ships, recruiting crew, and gathering supplies. All in all, it amounted to one of the most successful petitions of the many that were put forward in this period of imperial expansion. By comparison, Columbus had had to wait years for his project to finally gain approval from the Spanish crown, and Cortés had carried out his initial expedition into Mexico in defiance of the orders of the governor of Cuba.

Charles I (later Charles V of the Holy Roman Empire)

Nevertheless, the two captains soon met with their share of hindrances. From the start, the Spanish seafaring community was enraged when it learned that two Portuguese mariners had been awarded with such a lucrative set of concessions, and powerful figures at court soon set out to sabotage the expedition. Enemies of Magellan and Faleiro managed to hold up their funding in the Casa de Contratación, the royal office that administered the financing and organization of all such enterprises, and the entire mission was delayed. In the meantime, the Portuguese king, Manuel I, became aware of the deal Magellan had cut with his Spanish counterpart, and evidently came to regret having turned down the petitions of his former subject. He sent agents to Spain to attempt to derail the Portuguese captains. On top of that, internal problems between Magellan and Faleiro began to surface, creating further tension in their preparations. The clash of personalities ultimately led to Faleiro being stripped of his captaincy and left out of the mission.

Magellan was also prevented from recruiting many of his Portuguese acquaintances, despite the fact that some of them were already familiar with the territories they were setting out for, because the anti-Magellan factions in Spain managed to ensure that a large proportion of the crew and officers recruited were Spanish. Nevertheless, Magellan managed to take his longtime companion Enrique with him, and the crew that was finally assembled included men from a wide array of national backgrounds, including some North Africans.

By the time he was ready to sail, Magellan had five ships: the Trinidad (his flagship), the Victoria, the Concepcion, the Santo Antonio, and the Santiago. 273 men manned the 5 ships, 80% of whom were Spanish.

A replica of Magellan's *Victoria*

Chapter 9: Cortés and Pizarro Head to the New World

Hernán Cortés was born on an uncertain date in 1485 in Medellín, in the Spanish province of Extremadura. A dry, dusty, and hot backwater in the southwest of Spain, Extremadura was the home of many families of noble descent who had fallen into poverty, and it would prove to be the breeding ground of a majority of the conquistadors, most of whom came from honorable lineages but had few viable prospects in their native country. Indeed, this was the case for Hernán, son of Martín Cortés de Monroy and Catalina Pizarro Altamarino (through his mother, Cortés was a distant cousin of the conqueror of Peru, Francisco Pizarro). Though he is commonly referred to as Hernán today, he called himself Hernando or Fernando during his life.

The Spanish nobility was traditionally a warrior caste forged in the *reconquista*, the slow but ultimately successful reincorporation of the Iberian peninsula into Christendom at the expense of the Arabic-speaking Muslims who had ruled it for centuries. Cortés's father, a captain in the military, had remained true to the martial vocation of his class, but it held little tangible reward now that the Moors had been finally driven back into North Africa in 1492, the same year that Christopher Columbus first arrived in the New World thinking it was Asia.

Apparently a bright and ambitious child, Hernán Cortés left home for the prestigious University of Salamanca at the age of 14 with the intention of studying law. His parents, like many today, probably saw the legal profession as a steady and promising career path for their son, one which might help him restore the family's diminished fortune. But Cortés only remained at the university for two years, thus falling short of earning a degree. His evident impatience with the need for prolonged, sustained study reveals the restlessness and impetuousness that would become one of his most prevalent character traits. On the other hand, his legal studies provided him with knowledge that would later prove valuable when he was attempting to justify his claims to the land he conquered across the ocean and negotiate with the Spanish crown over his share of its wealth.

Thus, two of the qualities that Cortés would share with later conquistadors are evident from his early choices. First, he did not wish to follow a slow, gradual route to wealth and prominence; he wanted to achieve these things in a dramatic and immediate fashion. Second, he was willing to use the most influential forms of knowledge of the time and place, especially law and theology, to pursue his own aims, but he had no real reverence for learning in itself. His departure from Salamanca set a pattern. As he would do again and again, he left behind the old, the familiar, and established for the new, the uncertain, and the adventurous.

Spain's great writer Miguel de Cervantes, in a story about a man from Extremadura, described the Americas as "the refuge of the despairing sons of Spain, the church of the homeless, the asylum of homicides, the haven of gamblers and cheats, the general receptacle for loose women, the common center of attraction for many, but effectual resource of very few." As a contemporary view of the conquistadors and other arrivistes in the new colonies, Cervantes's is not a flattering portrait of what motivated men like Cortés to make the dangerous crossing of the Atlantic. And yet from what we know of his personality and early life, it seems like an accurate enough characterization of the man and the circles he frequented. A restless, mischievous young man, he found employment as a notary in the port city of Seville, but he soon found himself attracted to the new lands to the West, for which ships were departing regularly from Seville's harbor, and from which new wealth was arriving and remaking the city's economy.

When he departed for the island of Hispaniola in 1504, the memory of Columbus's discoveries was still fresh in the minds of the Spanish public. Columbus himself was still alive, but as a result of his disastrous stint as governor of Hispaniola, he had been relieved of his title of Viceroy of the Indies, and the crown had moved to centralize control over the new colonies and ensure their profitability. And though Columbus's voyage to the New World is remembered as one of the seminal events of the last millennium, at the time it still represented a bit of a disappointment. After all, Columbus's goal had been to reach Asia and ensure Spain's access to the trade in luxurious commodities such as spices and silk, and he had also hoped, later in his career, to reach the legendary gold mines of King Solomon.

Instead, what he had actually achieved was now uncertain, but it was becoming clear that rather than reaching the eastern edge of Asia, Columbus had arrived at a different land mass altogether. Justifying himself by the claim that the natives were barbaric heathens who needed to be civilized and converted to Christianity, Columbus had initiated a treatment of the native inhabitants that was at best paternalistic and at worst horrifically brutal and exploitative.

Making matters worse, Columbus had attempted to exploit the islands of Hispaniola and Cuba for gold only to find that the deposits were scarce. In the meantime, a system of thinly disguised slave labor came into being under the name of the *encomienda*, or "entrustment." The notion was that Spanish settlers would be granted a piece of land and power over the natives who inhabited it; their responsibility would be to instruct the natives in religion, in return for which "service" they could exact tributes of gold or other valuables, or labor in extractive or agricultural activities. The system laid the ground for the plantation-slave economy that would later become prevalent in the Caribbean.

It was into this environment that Cortés arrived in 1504, still not yet 20. Although Columbus had met with a friendly reception from the inhabitants of the islands he first visited, the conflict between Spanish settlers and natives had now become implacable. Understandably, the natives were not fond of the *encomienda* system or of the extreme savagery and cruelty of many Spaniards, and some had taken up arms against the new arrivals. One of Cortés's first experiences in the New World was to participate in expeditions against the remaining groups of Indians who had not yet been subjugated. It was here that he got his first taste of the casual brutality of the colonial frontier culture, as well as of the rewards that military exploits could bring. Through his military involvement, Cortés was granted a large *encomienda* in Hispaniola, including control over several hundred subjugated natives. In the meantime, he also offered his services as a notary and clerk to other settlers, establishing a fruitful set of relationships with the colonial authorities. Just over five years after arriving in the Indies, Cortés would move on from Hispaniola and take part in an expedition to Cuba, a larger island with far more as yet unconquered land.

Cortés's services to the new governor of Cuba, Diego Velázquez, earned him a prominent position in the new colony. He became clerk and secretary to the governor himself, gained control of a large *encomienda*, and accumulated enough prestige to become mayor of the city of Santiago. However, he soon got ahead of himself, amassing debts through an extravagant lifestyle and gaining the hostility of the governor on account of his unapologetic ambition and his seduction of the governor's sister-in-law, Catalina Juárez, whom Cortés ultimately married. Furthermore, he proved not to be a model citizen of the colony. According to chronicler Bernal Díaz del Castillo, who would accompany Cortés on his expedition to Mexico, the soon-to-be conquistador was a dandy, a lover of fineries, and unrestrained spender; despite his apparent wealth, Cortés accumulated vast debts during his years in Cuba through his luxurious lifestyle. Such a predicament provides a relatively banal explanation for his desire to set off and conquer new lands. If he was ever going to repay his creditors, he would need a windfall much bigger than the *encomienda* he had already acquired. By obtaining the title of Captain General, necessary for leading further expeditions, Cortés also obtained a higher credit limit, so to speak, because his creditors would now be guaranteed a share of any further profits he obtained.

Like Hernán Cortés and many other members of the front line of Spanish imperial expansion, Francisco Pizarro was born in the southwestern Spanish province of Extremadura. It was more or less the closest region geographically to the Indies, and due to its proximity to the great ports of Seville, Cádiz, and Lisbon, it had a more maritime and Atlantic orientation than the northern and eastern regions of Spain, which tended to look more to Europe and the Mediterranean. It was also a bone-dry and economically marginal region of greater than average poverty, where the experience of long-term war with the Moors and with Mediterranean rivals had created a frontier-like mentality and helped form a large class of men who sought their fortune in war rather than in commerce, the church, or courtly activity.

Francisco's father, Gonzalo Pizarro, belonged to this class and was an infantry officer with a relatively prestigious lineage who fought in a number of Mediterranean campaigns. His mother, on the other hand, was a poor woman who bore her son out of wedlock and later married another man, with whom she had several other sons. In part because of the humble circumstances of his birth and in part because of the general scarcity of birth records from the period, it is not clear exactly when Pizarro was born, although his birth occurred sometime in the 1470s and possibly in 1471. His city of origin was Trujillo, which would later become the name of a major city in Peru.

Pizarro was employed for some time as a swine herd in Spain, and as an uneducated illegitimate son he would have no inheritance and no likely prospects in the impoverished and stratified region where he grew up. Given that future, perhaps it was little surprise that he chose the same path as so many other Extremadurans with a poor outlook: the risky Atlantic passage to the New World. While the New World promised both wealth and glory for some, it also led many others to more debts and more disaster. Still, it is probably more surprising that he waited so long; if he was indeed born in 1471, he was nearly 40 by the time he set sail, and even if he was born as late as 1476, he was still well over 30. Cortés, in contrast, set out at the age of 19, having just barely left the university.

The two distant relatives, who had never met, arrived in the Indies within five years of each other: Cortés in 1504, Pizarro in 1509. Although much glory and fame was to accumulate to both names in the aftermath of their triumphs, for the most part the so-called "Indianos" (men who went to the Indies) had a poor reputation in Spain. They were regarded as greedy, ignoble, and unscrupulous types who put the pursuit of wealth before everything else, and for the most part this judgment seems to have been correct. Judging by their behavior upon arrival, the men who took part in the conquest were anything but admirable characters. Murder, rape, theft, and looting were all widespread activities in the ports from which they departed and the colonies themselves.

If he was in most regards less respectable than his distant cousin, Pizarro's initial trajectory in the New World differed from Cortés's in a related way. While Cortés had initially settled and taken up an administrative job in Hispaniola, the most established and centrally controlled of Spain's colonies at that point, Pizarro shipped out on an expedition to the northern edge of South America, a region still little explored by Spaniards and inhabited by mainly hostile tribes. His ship, under the command of Alonso de Ojeda, traveled along the coast of present-day Venezuela and Colombia before dropping anchor in the settlement of San Sebastián, which would later become the important port of Cartagena de Indias.

Depiction of Alonso de Ojeda

Pizarro quickly fell in with a crowd of restless, mutinously inclined men who had little patience with the established authorities. One of these was Vasco Núñez de Balboa, who had been in the Indies for some years and was evidently tired of deference and biding his time. He had owned property in Hispaniola but had profited little from it, and he had fallen into debt in the process. Balboa had sailed to the south both to escape his creditors and, like most other participants in the Spanish expeditions to the Indies, to try to secure a windfall that would solve his economic problems once and for all. It was with Balboa that Pizarro threw in his lot, and the ultimate consequences would be fateful.

Balboa would join the pantheon of conquistadors, though he is not remembered today for conquering anything. Balboa was, however, the first European to see the Pacific Ocean from the New World. Since it was the Pacific Ocean that Columbus originally sought to reach, this was a pivotal moment in the exploration and conquest of the Americas. Not coincidentally, Balboa reached the Pacific by crossing over the narrow piece of land that would one day become Panama, and which to this day serves via the Panama Canal as a crucial East-West conduit for trade. It was with Balboa that Panama first became a major geopolitical hotspot, not least because it was from there that Pizarro launched his missions down the western coast of South America. But prior to setting off across the isthmus, Balboa had established the city of Santa María del Darién, where both he and Pizarro established themselves as leading colonists.

Despite his accomplishments, Balboa was not appointed governor of the new settlement, and the position was instead given to Pedrarias Dávila, a veteran soldier of aristocratic background with close ties to the crown. A rivalry developed between the two men, and their conflict culminated in Dávila's execution of Balboa in 1519. By this point, Pizarro had established close ties with Dávila and had conspired against his former comrade Balboa. In exchange for his loyalty, Pizarro ascended in position, becoming mayor of Panama City and gaining a valuable land grant.

Chapter 10: Cortés's Conquest of the Aztecs

Expedition to the Mainland

Once he had gained his commission in 1518, Cortés wasted no time in gathering a fleet of ships and an army of ambitious followers, to whom he promised riches and land. In addition to permanently defraying his debts, Cortés now aimed to establish a permanent presence on the *terra firma*, which no Spaniard had yet accomplished since Columbus's failed attempt to colonize what is now Panama nearly 20 years earlier.

Cortés had little clear sense of what he would find, but rumors had long circulated about the existence of great empires with enormous treasures of gold. A previous expedition to the coastal Yucatán region of what is now Mexico had ended in failure, with the Spanish ambushed by local Mayans and the leader of the Spanish group injured. Certainly never averse to risk, Cortés was happy to take his chances with re-attempting the same expedition. Governor Velázquez, uneasy about Cortés's ambitions, attempted to restrict the newly minted Captain General from actually conquering and settling any territory, mandating that he should establish trade relations with the local inhabitants instead.

Velázquez apparently had an inkling of the fame and wealth that Cortés would achieve if he did manage to colonize the mainland and certainly did not trust Cortés to follow the orders he was given. When the fleet was nearly organized and ready to depart, the governor attempted twice to intervene and relieve Cortés of his leadership. Velázquez first sent a messenger whom Cortés promptly ordered killed, showing perhaps for the first time the full extent of his ruthlessness, and by the time Velázquez intervened a second time, Cortés was already just about to set sail and simply departed in direct defiance of his superior. Thus, when his 11 ships departed with a crew of over 500 men, they did so in open mutiny, taking advantage of the automatic delay that would be required for the governor to gather another expedition to go after them. Given that Cortés had invested a great deal of his personal wealth and gone into considerable debt to finance his excursion, it is not entirely surprising that he would behave with this degree of audacity. He likely sensed that he had lost the good will of Velázquez and would not be given another opportunity after this. Had he remained, he would have been at the mercy of his creditors and without any obvious way of turning his situation around, since he had already risen about as high as he was likely to in Cuba. His future was by no means guaranteed at this point, but he could be sure that he had few other options than to stake everything on success.

Sailing from the southeastern end of the island of Cuba in early 1519, the closest stretch of coast Cortés and his crew would find on the mainland was the Yucatán peninsula, once home to the large and wealthy Mayan empire. The Mayas had in recent centuries fragmented into smaller sub-groups and city states, and their wealth was now diminished. Previous Spaniards had found little success in the region, and Cortés probably set his sights somewhere else even before he landed, but he did spend some time on the island of Cozumel, just off the Yucatán coast.

Although he did not send a large land expedition into the peninsula, he acquired some of his most valuable assets there. First, he came across a Spaniard, survivor of a 1511 shipwreck, who had been living among the Mayas ever since. This man, Gerónimo de Aguilar, was now fluent in the Yucatec Mayan language, but he was also eager to return to his own people. Cortés took Aguilar in, and with that he had something that earlier conquistadors had lacked: a fully bilingual translator.

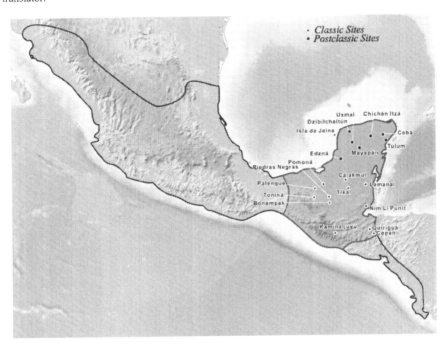

Map of the Mayan Empire

Aguilar's language skills, though, would have been of little use among the Nahuatl-speaking peoples further to the west had it not been for a second key encounter. On the other side of the Yucatán peninsula, Cortés was given possession of a young woman by the chief of another group of Mayas. This woman, it turned out, was a native of central Mexico and a fluent speaker of Nahuatl, as well as of Mayan and other languages. Cortés called her Doña Marina, but her original name was probably Malinalli, and she would later become known as Malintzin or Malinche to Mexicans. With the combined services of Aguilar and Doña Marina, Cortés now had the ability to communicate fluently with most of the peoples of Mexico, a capacity that gave him a crucial advantage in information gathering over earlier explorers such as Columbus, who proceeded with at-best rudimentary translation services, even in his later travels. Through the communicative chain he was able to establish, Cortés was able to find out not only the location of the great and wealthy Aztec empire, but also the resentment many neighboring tribes felt towards the Aztecs, a hostility he would make use of for his own purposes.

Cortes and La Malinche meet Moctezuma II in Tenochtitlan, November 8, 1519. Facsimile (c. 1890) of Lienzo de Tlaxcala.

Doña Marina, or Malinche, would play an outsized role in the conquest of Mexico. She ultimately became fluent in Spanish herself (diminishing Aguilar's importance), and was probably something of an advisor and confidant to Cortés. She was most certainly his mistress, and in 1522 she would bear him a son, Martín Cortés, often referred to as Mexico's first mestizo. The relationship would create tension with Cortés's Spanish wife, and Marina would be married off to another Spaniard. Still, her services earned her an *encomienda* and a relatively important status in the colony, and she was spoken of as a wise and graceful woman by Bernal Díaz and other chroniclers. Although the details of her later life are not known, she has become an iconic figure in Mexican history, sometimes a figure of pride, other times a figure of scorn and derision for her alleged betrayal of her native people and collaboration with the invading forces. However people choose to assess her actions, she was an extremely important figure whose participation in Cortés's expedition proved a crucial ingredient of its success.

The Aztec Empire

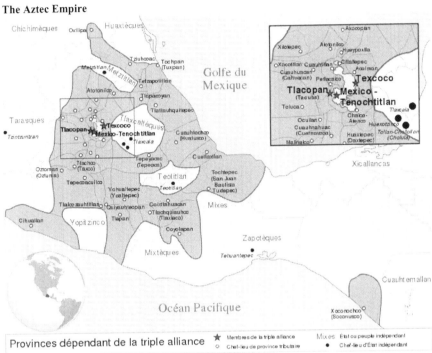

Provinces dépendant de la triple alliance

By the time he had made his way past the Yucatecan coast, Cortés seemed to know he wanted to reach what is to this day the Mexican heartland, the central valley of Mexico surrounding the city of Tenochtitlán. He had learned from many sources by now that this was the center of the region's most powerful and wealthy empire. If the reports proved true, Cortés knew, he would be able to accomplish something that had eluded previous Spanish explorers. When Columbus had set out in 1492, his goal was to establish contact with the great urban empires of Asia, places of immense wealth and sophistication. Instead, he had found a series of islands populated by people who were remarkable poor and simple by European standards. They did not live in cities or practice large-scale commerce or even possess more than small quantities of gold. If the Aztecs proved as wealthy as he had been told, Cortés would succeed where Columbus had failed. Within this context, his continued defiance of the orders of the colonial authorities makes sense: a conquest of the scale he was envisioning would so impress the Spanish crown that both his infractions and his debts would be instantly forgiven.

Cortés's reports were accurate: the Aztecs – also called the Mexica – did stand at the helm of an immense, sophisticated, and wealthy empire. Like the Spaniards, they had expanded their territories through a vertiginous process of territorial conquest. Surprisingly, given their vast power, the Aztecs had only risen to importance about a hundred years before Cortés arrived in their territory, but they had built on the architectural, religious, and military achievements of a sequence of earlier empires such as the Olmecs and Toltecs, and they had created a powerful network of alliances among the city states of the valley of Mexico. They now controlled a large portion of the central region of what is now Mexico, territories that stretched from the northern deserts to the southern rainforests and from the gulf of Mexico to the Pacific Ocean.

The territory over which the Aztecs held control expanded quickly under the rule of the all powerful kings. This was the period of what has been called the Aztec Empire, though calling it an empire is somewhat a misnomer. Unlike other historical empires, the Aztecs did not actually occupy or govern the people they conquered within their empire. When they conquered a city, the Aztecs acquired captives and the right to tribute, which was to be sent to Tenochtitlan according to a regular schedule. Since the Aztecs did not leave behind administrators or a garrison but merely went home with their captives, it was left up to the conquered city to render tribute when it was due. Those cities that reneged would be subject to a renewed attack in which more captives were taken and more tribute was demanded. Making this arrangement even more unique, the Aztecs did not maintain a standing army; their empire was controlled or policed by warriors assembled on an ad hoc basis. That they proved so successful and conquered such a large area is all the more remarkable.

The Aztecs' expansion was out of necessity. When Tenochtitlan suffered food shortages caused by increased population and/or crop failures, their warriors were dispatched to subjugate new territories and win more tribute. Of course, as time went on the new tribute cities were located further and further away from the capital, and the Aztecs found the land to the west and north was not productive enough to warrant imperial expansion. To the south, the tribute cities provided luxury goods but were too far distant to provide a source for food. So it was to the east that the Aztecs began expanding their empire. But the increasing distances of the tribute cities made the food distribution system less and less efficient as the empire expanded, because the Aztecs lacked wheeled vehicles and customary beasts of burden.

As a result, the Aztecs had to rely on human porters to transport the incoming tribute, which posed a unique problem of its own. The further these human porters had to carry food, the more of it they consumed along the way. Thus, the most important cities within the empire that supplied food to the Aztecs were within easy reach of Lake Texcoco.

Another important aspect of the transportation system was the fact that the Aztecs' capital was literally on an island, which required using water for travel and transportation. Plying the waters of lagoons or lakes in the Valley of Mexico, there were as many as 10,000 canoes, some as long as 50 feet. These vessels brought goods across Lake Texcoco from lakeshore farms and villages, as well as tribute carried from more distant vassal towns.

Perhaps most problematically, they demanded hundreds or even thousands of captives be sent every year to be sacrificed in the festivals of their patron deities. Such practices had earned the hostility of several of the neighboring regions. Since the Aztecs did not have a significant military presence outside of their immediate territory around the city of Tenochtitlán, this rendered them highly vulnerable to invasion if one of their tributary groups chose to take the side of the invader. That is precisely what would happen when Cortés and his men arrived.

Before that, however, Cortés had to ensure that he would have no further trouble from his superiors in Cuba. To achieve the autonomy he sought, he took two major steps. First, upon arriving to the stretch of the Gulf Coast nearest to the Aztec heartland, he established the city of Veracruz, complete with a mayor and city council drawn from among his men. By way of this legal sleight of hand, Cortés could claim that he no longer needed to report to the governor of Cuba, since the legitimate authorities of an independent city reported directly to Charles V, the King of Spain. Cortés may not have finished studying the law, but he was clearly putting it to use here. Second, Cortés took the dramatic step of burning his ships in the harbor, signaling that he and his men would not be returning any time soon. Once again, the action suggests a remarkable impetuousness and willingness to gamble for high stakes.

Charles V

In the meantime, Cortés began to establish contact both with local tribes, some of whom expressed to him their frustration with Aztec rule, and with emissaries of the Aztec emperor, Motecuhzoma (also known as Moctezuma or Montezuma). In the meantime, it was by no means certain that the ploy to elude Velázquez's authority would actually work, since it was possible that the Spanish crown would refuse to acknowledge Cortés's new settlement, but it would take months for news of Cortés's actions to reach Spain, and it would be several more before orders returned to Cortés himself.

The Spaniards bided their time on the coast for some weeks, exchanging messages with the Aztecs and attempting to glean more information before proceeding, since they still had little sense of the exact scale of the kingdom they were planning to take on. When Moctezuma became aware of the strangers in his territory, he responded in a mainly friendly and hospitable manner, repeatedly sending them gifts and inviting them to remain on the land if they were willing to move their settlement somewhat further away from the capital. Not surprisingly, the Spaniards refused that offer.

Historians have long speculated as to why Moctezuma was so generous and unsuspicious toward the invaders who would soon bring about his demise. One popular claim is that the arrival of Cortés and his men coincided with a long-prophesied return of the god Quetzalcoatl, said to be a light-haired and light-skinned being who would arrive from across the sea; Moctezuma's deference, in this account, would be the result of his fear that he was dealing with a god rather than a man. However, more recent analysis has suggested that the Quetzalcoatl legend was developed after the conquest, specifically as a way for the Aztec elite to explain the sudden and traumatic liquidation of their entire world. A more reasonable explanation may be based on local politics: Moctezuma knew that his rule was vulnerable and that he had many rivals in and out of Tenochtitlán, so he may have hoped to keep the strangers loyal to him lest they provide aid to his enemies.

If that was the case, Moctezuma actually proved quite prescient, because this is exactly the approach Cortés adopted. He made contact with several of the tribes that deeply resented Aztec rule and promised to support them in a war against their oppressors. What Moctezuma did not seem prepared for, though, was Cortés's endless capacity for treachery and duplicity. He remained in apparently friendly contact with Moctezuma for weeks, accepting gifts and sending more in exchange, even as he was steadily building up an army of indigenous allies who would help him take on the Aztecs. All evidence suggests that Moctezuma was a deeply honorable ruler who remained committed to basic rules and principles of decency and hospitality, and to his detriment he seemed to assume that these new arrivals would behave similarly. But Cortés, as his interactions with Velázquez have already demonstrated, had little use for deference to authority and did not consider customs worth much. His cynical act of establishing a city in order to circumvent the governor's authority suggests Cortés saw rules and laws as things to be manipulated in order to pursue his goals. He took the same approach in his interactions with the Aztec ruler.

Religion provided another fruitful area for Cortés's manipulations. While still on the Gulf Coast, he began attempting to evangelize the native inhabitants – essentially demanding that they accept Christianity or face the consequences. Given what is known of his unscrupulous character, it is difficult to imagine that the conquistador earnestly wished to bring these people to the true faith. But religion proved useful to him in several ways. For one, it allowed him to sanctify a mission that otherwise seemed transparently motivated by greed and egotism. This would prove particularly helpful in gaining royal support back in Spain, since the most widely accepted justification for conquests was that they were a way of spreading the faith. After all, this principle was at the basis of the *encomienda* system, since the holder of an encomienda was charged with instructing his subordinates in religion. Second, the natives understood from their own belief system that to accept a conqueror's rule also included accepting the conqueror's god. When Cortés and his men destroyed the native idols in a temple and replaced them with crucifixes and virgins, it was above all a gesture of power. Third, and even more cynically, religion provided a pretext for unleashing violence. When natives refused to accept the gospel and persisted in their allegedly satanic practices, Cortés used this recalcitrance as a justification for attacking and killing them, since rejection of Christ could be presented as an act of aggression equivalent to war. Several of the most brutal massacres against unarmed people he and his men carried out were performed in the midst of rituals, so that they could claim that they had used force to prevent their victims from carrying out their pagan rites. Cortés was adept at rhetorical displays of piety, but his behavior in war was so craven and so blatantly un-Christian that many contemporaries, including the king himself, had some trouble swallowing his protestations.

Having established alliances with several of the coastal peoples, while still remaining in contact with Aztec emissaries and holding out for a requested meeting with Moctezuma, Cortés eventually marched inland toward Tenochtitlán. He departed with about three hundred of his own men, plus several hundred Totonac allies, leaving another hundred or so Spaniards behind in Veracruz. Along the way he encountered another people which had long rejected the legitimacy of Aztec rule: the Tlaxcalans or Tlaxcaltecas. They were a particularly warlike people, as the Spaniards discovered in a series of skirmishes with them. It appears that both groups concluded, after a series of meetings between Spanish and Tlaxcalan emissaries, that each could make use of the other in a common war against the Aztecs.

Although it is not clear at this point that Cortés already intended to undertake an immediate war against Moctezuma and his people, the Tlaxcalan alliance would prove crucial in everything that followed. Indeed, by the time the Spaniards left Tlaxcala, they were accompanied by about 3,000 Tlaxcalan warriors, approximately three times the size of the Spanish force itself. This fact, as historian Matthew Restall has argued, puts to rest the myth of a tiny army of Spaniards defeating a great empire; in reality, the Spanish expedition would have almost certainly been routed without a massive contingent of allies.

With his large assembled forces in tow, Cortés proceeded onward to the city of Cholula, second only to the capital of Tenochtitlán in scale. Its inhabitants were traditionally close allies of the Aztecs and enemies of the Tlaxcalans, so the arrival of a large army of their rivals no doubt caused some unease. Nevertheless, the newcomers were welcomed into the city, and Cortés requested an audience with the king and other notables. What followed was a kind of rehearsal for the treachery and brutality that would then be practiced on a larger scale in the capital. Having invited the chief authorities of the city into a public square, they ambushed the crowd of hundreds of unarmed people gathered there, killing in one audacious stroke the entire leadership of the city as well as much of its warrior class. Cortés subsequently claimed that he had received word, through Doña Marina, that some of the Cholulans were plotting with a nearby Aztec regiment to massacre the Spaniards, and that they had acted in self-defense. Historians find this implausible, and have sought other explanations. One is that the massacre was carried out at the behest of the Tlaxcalans, who had their own agenda to pursue against their rivals. Another is that Cortés's main purpose was to instill fear in the local inhabitants in general and Moctezuma and his advisors in particular.

Spaniards and Aztecs in Tenochtitlán

Today Tenochtitlan is mostly remembered for being a floating island city, made all the more ironic by the fact that it was essentially the forerunner of Mexico City, one of the biggest cities in the world today. Lake Texcoco was part of a closed river basin consisting of shallow lakes, lagoons and marshes that formed during the period of glaciation and received additional waters during the annual rainy season. It was on this lake that the floating city was created.

Because the existence of Tenochtitlan depended on water management for the safety of the city, the Aztecs developed ingenius waterworks to facilitate agriculture and the movement of goods. Aqueducts supplied the drinking water, while canals, wharves and flood control gates enabled reliable waterborne commerce. The Aztecs maintained control of the input of water into the lakes and marshes, keeping the salt content of the otherwise closed system under control. Though they accomplished this with hard labor, the Aztecs ensured that Tláloc, the god of water who controlled rain and storms, was content, with one of the two elevated sanctuaries on the great central pyramid of Tenochtitlan was dedicated to Tláloc.

Fresh water was first supplied to the city by means of two channels made of reeds and mud that ran from Chapultepec, and reservoirs were constructed in Tenochtitlan from which residents obtained their water for household use. The two channels also delivered water to underground aqueducts that supplied the palaces of the elite in the center of the city. The running water was used to supply the many baths in the palaces, as well as pools and irrigated gardens.

At the height of the Aztec empire, a more ambitious aqueduct was constructed between Chapultepec and the city, spanning nearly 10 miles. This aqueduct was over 20 feet wide. As the city grew further and more water was required, another elaborate aqueduct was constructed in 1499 to bring water from five springs that fed into a dammed basin in Coyoacán. Lacking a control mechanism to prevent exceptional water flow from coursing down the spill way into the city, the aqueduct actually proved to be a hazard to the inhabitants of Tenochtitlan. In 1500, when there were unprecedented rains, the city suffered a disastrous flood partly due to the rising water level in Lake Texcoco but more importantly from this unstoppable aqueduct.

The Aztecs used a considerable amount of water for bathing and washing their streets, with thousands of laborers watering and sweeping the streets daily. The elite classes also kept themselves clean by using soap to bathe, and according to the Spanish, Montezuma bathed twice a day in tubs in the royal palace. He apparently changed his clothes frequently as well.

The Aztecs were meticulous in the control of waste. No solid waste was disposed of through the drainage pipes that emptied into the lake. Care was taken to collect solid waste and what was appropriate was taken to the chiampas for use as fertilizer.

By the time Tenochtitlan was taken by the Spanish, it spanned some 1,000 hectares, the equivalent of 10 million square meters. The incredible size and organization of Tenochtitlan was so impressive to the conquistadors that some of them compared it to Venice. The population size also astonished the conquistadors, who found one well organized market in which 60,000 people were carrying on business. The market had a huge variety of goods for exchange, and nearby were a number of studios where highly skilled artisans worked and sold their goods.

The city centered on the walled square of the Great Temple and adjacent residences of the king, priests and elite warriors. The streets were laid out in a grid pattern interspersed by canals in each of the quarters and their constituent calpulli or wards. Causeways connected the city to the mainland, alongside which ran the aqueducts.

Ruins of Templo Mayor

In the center of Tenochtitlan was a walled precinct. The wall was decorated on the outside with snakes, earning it the name *coatepantli* or serpent wall. It contained a large square, the enormous pyramidal Templo Mayor. The Templo Mayor or Great Temple was rebuilt several times over, with the new and improved structure simply constructed over the previous and less elevated pyramid. The last version of the Templo Mayor was dedicated in 1487 and reached a height of about 130 feet.

The pyramid was capped by two temples, with one dedicated to Huizilopochtli and the other to

Tláloc. The idea of capping a pyramid with twin temples was derived from earlier post classic construction at such sites as Tula and Teotihuacán. Though the Mayans are the ones remembered for their mastery of astronomy, the Aztecs' temples were oriented in such a way as to emphasize the seasonal movement of the sun. In the wetter season, the sun rose behind the Temple of Tláloc, and in the summer it rose behind the Temple of Huizilopochtli. On the two equinoctial days the sun rose between the two temples and shone on the Temple of Quetzalcoatl that faced the Templo Mayor.

In the walled central temple enclosure there were five other structures. Among them were the Temple of Xipe Totec and the Temple of Tezcatlipoca. Included in the central temple enclosure was also a ball court where it is presumed religiously based athletic competitions were held. The exact nature of the Aztec ball game is unknown, but it is likely that it was similar to that in other Mesoamerican cities and involved teams hitting a ball through a goal using their hips or chests or heads.

The common people of Tenochtitlan lived in houses that fronted on the streets of their calpulli. The adobe or wattle and daub houses were L-shaped, enclosing an interior courtyard in which most of the domestic activities were carried out. Here the women spun thread and wove fabric, ground corn, baked tortillas, prepared food and interacted with kin who came and went with little formality. The domestic court was the site of family festivals celebrating the birth or naming of a child, in which quantities of food were given to friends, neighbors and the hungry poor. The common men worked on their chinampas or fished in the lake.

Estimates of the population of Tenochtitlan vary considerably, but it is likely that the total population of the city was in the range of 200,000 to 300,000 most of which would have been of the common class. It is probable that the second largest segment of the population were slaves. The sheer number of people in Tenochtitlan amazed the conquistadors, who compared the size of the city to some of the largest municipalities at home in Spain. Incredibly, the city had amenities that were unthought of even in Europe. For example, there were schools for children of all classes, even commoners. Adjacent to the local temple the schools provided instruction for children from 7 to 14 years in age with boys and girls taught in separate rooms. Children were taught the history of the Aztecs, dancing, singing, public speaking and were even given religious instruction. The schools for children of the elite were located in the center of Tenochtitlan. There they were taught a broader curriculum that included astronomy, arithmetic, oratory, reading and writing.

Regardless of the precise population count, when Cortés and his men arrived in Tenochtitlán, it was probably larger than any European city of the era. Bernal Díaz, who accompanied Cortés, describes the reaction of the Spanish soldiers as they first approached the great city: "We saw so many cities and villages built both on the water and on dry land, and a straight, level causeway (to Tenochtitlan), we couldn't resist our admiration. It was like the enchantments in the book of Amadis (de Gaula, a popular Spanish chivalric romance of the late middle ages), because of the high towers, pyramids and other buildings, all of masonry, which rose from the water. Some of our soldiers asked if what we saw was not a dream."

This was the first great urban civilization that the Spaniards, who had initially come to the Americas seeking the rich and sophisticated kingdoms of Asia, encountered in the New World. It is a remarkable fact that within less than two years of their first arrival there, Tenochtitlán as they had found it would be in ruins. It is not entirely clear to what extent this outcome should be attributed to the ruthlessness and irreverence of the Spanish expedition's leader, but Cortés surely bears a great deal of responsibility for what occurred.

The combined Spanish and Tlaxcalan force of several thousand entered the Aztec capital on November 8, 1519. They were prepared for battle, but initially met a peaceful reception. Moctezuma, as he had previously done on several occasions through emissaries, presented the visitors with lavish gifts, including objects forged from gold, which surely whetted the Spaniards' appetite. They were welcomed into the city and brought into its central palace complex. Many have wondered why an apparently hostile army was treated with such hospitality, especially after the massacre at Cholula. One theory is that Moctezuma simply did not imagine that such a small force could be a threat to his enormous city. Once the strangers were ensconced in the city, he may have reasoned, they were trapped and would have great difficulty escaping. Once again, even if this was his intention, the Aztec ruler severely underestimated his opponent. Not long after arriving in Tenochtitlán, apparently prompted by a report that his men back in Veracuz had been attacked by the Aztecs, Cortés took Moctezuma hostage in his own palace. The ruler showed little resistance, and allowed the Spaniards to plunder the royal storehouses of gold. For several months, Cortés essentially ruled Tenochtitlán through the authority of his captive, not establishing decisive control there but biding his time until a more forceful move could be taken.

However, Cortés still had the authorities of his own government to deal with as well. In April 1520, a Spanish expedition of around 1,000 men under the command of Pánfilo de Narváez was sent out by Governor Velázquez from Cuba with orders to subdue Cortés. Here again Cortés was severely outnumbered, but his ruthlessness won out. Leaving Tenochtitlán and heading for the coast, Cortés feigned a desire to enter into peace talks, holding out a promise of consensual submission to the governor's authority. All the while, he was planning to attack and sending messengers to Narváez's camp with bribes and promises of rewards if they mutinied against their appointed leader. Narváez was unprepared when Cortés and his men descended on the encampment fully armed and ready to fight. He was forced to surrender and fell captive to his enemy, who left him imprisoned in Veracruz while leading off a large contingent of his soldiers back toward Tenochtitlán. It is an interesting fact that Cortés did not reserve his treacherous disregard for basic honesty for his interactions with the natives. He behaved with similar callousness toward his own people, albeit with much less brutality, but even that might have been only because he did not have to resort to brute force.

While Cortés was dealing with fellow Spaniards, the group of Spaniards in Tenochtitlán had meanwhile carried out a massacre as shocking and probably with more even bloodshed than the one in Cholula. Cortés's lieutenant Pedro de Alvarado was immediately responsible for planning and ordering the attack, but it is not clear whether he was acting under orders from his superior or on his own initiative. Some speculate that Cortés deliberately planned for it to occur during his absence so that he could claim to have been uninvolved. The occasion of the massacre was the festival of Toxatl, which celebrated the god Tezcatlipoca and was probably the largest and most important of all Aztec feast days. The nobles and priests of the city were gathered in the courtyard of the great Templo Mayor, which could only be accessed through four narrow entrances. With his small group of Spaniards, Alvarado sealed off the exits and in the midst of the celebration, entered into the courtyard and began slaughtering the gathered Aztecs, all of them unarmed. They are thought to have killed thousands, possibly as many as eight thousand, that day, primarily using swords, spears, and knives. As in Cholula, the perpetrators later claimed that they had gotten wind of a plot against them by the Aztecs; they also claimed that they were acting to prevent the participants in the festival from carrying out rituals involving human sacrifice and cannibalism.

Pedro de Alvarado

It's no surprise that the Spaniards would use the Aztec human sacrifice rituals as a pretext to justify their aggression. More is known about Aztec religious practices than any other aspect of their culture, mostly because the major element in the public ceremonies was focused on human sacrifice. The rituals were apparently so gruesome that they horrified even the Spanish, who were not exactly known for their gentility when it came to war and religious fervor.

Although some have suggested other theories to explain the large amount of human sacrifices, including political intimidation and even as a means of population control, it is still widely believed that they had religious symbolism. Thus, the Aztecs, either to please the gods or ensure their constant attention to earthly life, frequently bestowed on them the gift of sacrificial humans. This in itself was not unique to the region, as it was a well documented practice among other Mesoamerican civilizations. In fact, the Aztecs' enemy, the Tlaxcala, sacrificed captured Aztecs, and some of their accounts suggest it was considered an honor to die as a sacrifice. And human sacrifice in and of itself would not have been particularly upsetting to the Spanish, nor would it have been of great interest to generations of readers on the Aztecs.

However, the brutality, quantity and method of disposal of human remains as practiced by the Aztecs almost defy the imagination. An example of the rite of human sacrifice at its height was that performed for the dedication of the new Templo Mayor in 1487. The ceremony lasted four days, during which anywhere from 4,000 to 20,000 humans were sacrificed. As proof of their zeal, Aztec accounts themselves placed the number over 80,000, which would have required sacrificing over a dozen people a minute. Captives from the Huastec region to the east of Tenochtitlan were paraded through the temple square joined by ropes threaded through their pierced noses. They climbed one by one up the steep steps of the pyramid to the temples at the top where they were laid over a stone. A priest wielding an obsidian-bladed ritual knife hacked open the victim's chest, tore out the still beating heart and placed it in a basin where it was incinerated. The body of the victim was kicked off the temple platform and rolled down to the square below. Here it was dismembered. The skull was installed on a rack and the limbs were distributed to the crowd assembled in the square.

**Temple Sacrifice. Codex Magliabechiano, mid 16th century based on an earlier codex.
Biblioteca Nazionale Centrale, Florence**

The ceremonial dedication of the Templo Mayor may have been on a grander scale than day to day ritual sacrifice, but the number of victims of Aztec religious practices was always high. When Cortés' men were shown into the temples of Tenochtitlan in 1519, they were nauseated by the stench of the burning hearts and the blood soaked walls. Bernal Diaz described what he saw in one of the temples. On these altars were idols, with evil looking bodies, he reported, and every night five captives were sacrificed before them. Their chests were cut open, and their arms and thighs were cut off. The walls of the temple were covered with blood. "We stood greatly amazed and gave the island the name *isleta de Sacrificios* (Island of the Sacrifices)."

Describing one sacrifice in detail, he wrote:

"They strike open the wretched Indian's chest with flint knives and hastily tear out the palpitating heart which, with the blood, they present to the idols [...]. They cut off the arms, thighs and head, eating the arms and thighs at ceremonial banquets. The head they hang up on a beam, and the body is [...] given to the beasts of prey."

The beasts of prey were the animals in Montequma's zoo. Diaz continues:

"They have a most horrid and abominable custom which truly ought to be punished and which until now we have seen in no other part, and this is that, whenever they wish to ask something of the idols, in order that their plea may find more acceptance, they take many girls and boys and even adults, and in the presence of these idols they open their chests while they are still alive and take out their hearts and entrails and burn them before the idols, offering the smoke as sacrifice. Some of us have seen this, and they say it is the most terrible and frightful thing they have ever witnessed."

The victims taken to Tenochtitlan were well taken care of before suffering their fate. Warriors might claim a special victim that they had personally captured, and that captive would be well fed and tended in a cage. When he was dispatched by the priest, his limbs would be given to the warrior who had captured him. The warrior, who would have been among the 400 men put forth by each calpulli and who fought under a ward banner, celebrated his skill by inviting a number of people to join him in partaking of the special meal. The poor might also crowd into the party in the hopes that some scraps would be given to them.

The execution of captives varied depending on the god to which they were sacrificed. For example, in the temple dedicated to Mixocoatl, the god of hunting, a victim was shot full of arrows before his heart was removed and he was dismembered.

The festival of Tlacaxipehualiztli (flaying of men), celebrated annually just before the rainy season, was held at the temple of Xipe Totec, "our lord the flayed one", the sun god. The victims who had been well treated, perhaps even revered prior to the festival, were dressed in costumes to appear like Xipe Totec. They were tied to large stones and armed with feather encrusted weapons to fight off the advances of five warriors who were armed with spears and obsidian bladed clubs. The blood of the victims fed the earth and ensured a good planting season. The victims' bodies were flayed, and the priests of the temple wore their skins for 20 days.

The Aztecs clearly had a stomach for blood and death, but the massacre during a celebratory festival by the Spaniards definitively exhausted their toleration of the invaders, who despite the thousands they killed were still outnumbered and highly vulnerable under siege. Word of the massacre spread, and the city's inhabitants rose up against their would-be rulers, driving them back into Moctezuma's palace, where they were protected only by the presence of their venerated hostage. Meanwhile, Cortés was made aware by messengers of the latest events and made haste toward the capital with his enlarged force of Spaniards and a contingent of Tlaxcalan allies.

When they arrived, they found the city's streets deserted and the population openly hostile. What ensued was a kind of prototype of urban guerrilla warfare. In the tight, enclosed spaces of the city, the Spaniards' horses were of little advantage, and their weapons could not be fired effectively. Within a short period, it became clear that they had lost their advantage, and they were running low on food and artillery. Cortés's gambit was to have Moctezuma, still his captive, speak to his people, ostensibly in the hope of a further reconciliation. Having ascended to the roof of his palace to speak to the assembled Aztecs, Moctezuma was killed under circumstances that still remain uncertain. The Spaniards subsequently claimed that he was stoned to death by his own people, while the native accounts mainly assert that the Spaniards themselves killed the emperor, literally stabbing him in the back while he tried to speak. Both scenarios are relatively plausible, but the latter explanation certainly fits with Cortés's style.

The retreat that followed after Moctezuma's death has become known as the *Noche triste* ("sad night," "night of sorrow"), although the Aztecs were presumably not sorry to see the Spaniards go or even terribly sorry for the loss of their ineffectual ruler. Cortés and his men, knowing they were badly outnumbered and had little chance of surviving open combat in the city, chose to flee after sending a false message of truce to their enemies. They fled in the middle of the night, aiming for the most deserted causeway leading out of the city and across the lake, but the retreat still went disastrously. It began to rain heavily, thunderstorms added to their consternation, and all out chaos ensued when they were attacked by large numbers of their opponents, who had been alerted to their movements. Many of the Spaniards were weighted down with gold and other loot from the city and drowned when they tried to swim away from the causeway, while others were simply killed by the attackers. All in all, hundreds of them did not escape the city alive, leaving the force greatly diminished. By the time Cortés reached the shores of the lake, he had lost most of his army and much of the treasure he and his men had taken from Moctezuma's palace. His initial plan to take control of the Aztec empire by stealth, keeping Moctezuma on the throne as a nominal leader while ruling from behind the scenes, had failed disastrously. Now he would need to try a different and far more dramatic strategy.

Even after clearing the causeway, the retreating Spaniards were pursued by their Aztec enemies and engaged in repeated skirmishes as they fled toward Tlaxcala to reconvene with allies there. In the valley of Otumba, they were attacked by a large Aztec force and a bloody battle followed. Despite being outnumbered, the Spaniards ultimately beat back their opponents, partly because of the superior speed and agility provided by their horses, which had proved much less of an asset in the urban setting of Tenochtitlán. Their equivocal victory at Otumba allowed them to proceed on toward the east, but they lost many more men, both Spaniards and native allies, in the fighting. By the time they arrived in Tlaxcala, nearly 900 Spanish soldiers and more than a thousand native allies had perished. In their weakened position and having failed in their first campaign, the Spaniards were in a weaker bargaining position with their allies, who demanded further concessions in exchange for continued support. Cortés was willing to grant the Tlaxcalans much of what they requested, including control of previously held Aztec territories as tributary regions, and partial control of Tenochtitlán itself. In exchange, he obtained an army of allies who had even more stake in victory and thus higher morale.

The Fall of Tenochtitlán

Tenochtitlán had been left in a chaotic state, and although Cuitláhuac had been appointed as a successor for Moctezuma, his authority was not yet fully consolidated. Traditionally Aztec rulers were required to demonstrate their prowess by leading an army into battle and taking captives, who would then be sacrificed to the gods upon his return. The military venture would also serve the purpose of confirming his effective leadership and obtaining the continued loyalty of tributary states. However appropriate it may have seemed to take an army to Tlaxcala to confront the Spaniards and their allies there, Cuitláhuac was formally prohibited from leading a full military campaign because the season for such activities had not yet arrived: most able-bodied men were supposed to be harvesting food rather than fighting. Only when the winter came would it be possible to assemble a large military force.

On the other hand, there was a certain strategic advantage to remaining in Tenochtitlán, since it seemed an easy position to fortify and defend given its location on the lake: any advancing army would have to cross the narrow causeways, and as the Spaniards had already discovered, this would make them easy targets. For one of these reasons, or perhaps all of them, the Aztecs hung back for the moment, as did the Spaniards, who sent for reinforcements from Veracruz and Cuba and went about building support from several smaller cities in the Tlaxcalan sphere of influence.

By the time the Aztecs sent out expeditionary forces to attack the Spaniards in the Fall of 1520, the Spaniards had gathered an impressive array of support from native allied forces, and their own resources had augmented thanks to a growing trickle of soldiers, horses, and artillery arriving from the Gulf of Mexico. Still, the army that finally gathered to re-enter the Valley of Mexico toward the end of that same year was less than 5% Spanish, and it is unlikely that most of the native soldiers who participated regarded themselves as under Cortés's command. The traditional view of the "Spanish Conquest" thus needs to be revised. Although the Spaniards ultimately derived the most benefit from the war against the Aztecs, most of the participants in the successful campaign were neither Spanish nor conquerors: they were pursuing an agenda that would ostensibly increase their city's share of regional power. A further and equally crucial actor in the ultimate triumph of the Spaniards was one of the diseases they had brought with them from Europe: smallpox. By late 1520, a devastating outbreak of the illness had ravaged Tenochtitlán, killing perhaps 40% of its population. One of the victims was Cuitláhuac, who fell ill and died in early December, meaning that the Aztecs were without a leader at a time in which they should have been marshaling forces for war. The succession was controversial, and the next chosen king, Cuahtemoc, was not officially recognized until February of 1521. By this time, the

Spaniards had returned and had a number of new advantages.

With a greatly enlarged contingent of native allies, hundreds of reinforcements from Cuba, and a refreshed stock of arquebuses, cannons, and gunpowder, Cortés now headed toward Tenochtitlán with a far superior force than he had previously. Even still, he did not proceed immediately to the city but set out to consolidate his control of the surrounding region, establishing alliances where possible and subduing cities and towns where necessary. The aim was to isolate the Aztecs, cut off their supplies of food and fresh water from neighboring territories, and prevent them from being able to summon reinforcements. The strategy was effective, and the result was a tightening noose around the already diminished, divided, and illness-ravaged Aztec populations. Cortés also arrived at Lake Texcoco with brigantines that allowed his forces to cross the lake and attack the city without needing to use the causeways. But for the most part, he and his allies waged a defensive war.

Once the supply chain had been cut off and food and water were scarce in the city, the Aztecs' only recourse was to go out and try to fend off the siege, thus leaving themselves vulnerable to attacks from their enemies. But despite mass starvation, the Aztecs held out and continued to prevent any major advances on their city for months.

Finally, in July, the Spaniards and their allies managed to gain a foothold on the island, and proceeded to make their way through the city, razing structures to the ground to prevent ambushes. Worn down by illness, starvation, thirst, and relentless arquebus and cannon attacks, the Aztecs held out until August 13, 1521, the day Cuahtemoc was captured. He reportedly surrendered directly to Cortés, but his surrender was not recognized and he was taken prisoner and ultimately executed. The total numbers are uncertain, but Aztec casualties from the siege, including the deaths of warriors in battle and deaths from illness, starvation, and massacres of civilians, reached the hundreds of thousands. In the latest stage of their campaign, the Spaniards had lost perhaps 500 and native allies had perished in the tens of thousands. Within less than two years, the Aztec empire had been destroyed, the population decimated, and the great capital left in ruins. Cortés proceeded to take credit for the entire enterprise, but in reality his success was highly dependent on the enormous assistance he received from his local allies. Perhaps more than a great military strategist, he had again shown himself to be a consummate politician.

Chapter 11: Magellan's Expedition

As it turned out, Cortés would conduct his historic conquest of the Aztecs at precisely the same time Magellan was seeking a route through South America to the Spice Islands. Of all the historic and famous expeditions made during the Age of Exploration, it's no exaggeration to say that Magellan's was the most unique and adventurous. Ironically, Magellan's expedition is taught to schoolchildren across the globe, but his fate during the voyage itself is not. As a result, much of what is known about the expedition came from the journal of one of the crew, Antonio Pigafetta:

"Finding myself in Spain in the year of the nativity of our Lord, 1519, at the court of the most serene King of the Romans (Charles V), and learning there of the great and awful things of the ocean world, I desired to make a voyage to unknown seas, and to see with my own eyes some of the wonderful things of which I had heard.

I heard that there was in the city of Seville an armada (armade) of five ships, which were ready to perform a long voyage in order to find the shortest way to the Islands of Moluco (Molucca) from whence came the spices. The Captain General of this armada was Ferdinand de Magagleanes (Magellan), a Portuguese gentleman, who had made several voyages on the ocean. He was an honorable man. So I set out from Barcelona, where the Emperor was, and traveled by land to the said city of Seville, and secured a place in the expedition.

The Captain General published ordinances for the guidance of the voyage.

He willed that the vessel on which he himself was should go before the other vessels, and that the others should keep in sight of it. Therefore he hung by night over the deck a torch or faggot of burning wood which he called a farol (lantern), which burned all night, so that the ships might not lose sight of his own.

He arranged to set other lights as signals in the night. When he wished to make a tack on account of a change of weather he set two lights. Three lights signified "faster." Four lights signified to stop and turn. When he discovered a rock or land, it was to be signalled by other lights.

He ordered that three watches should be kept at night.

On Monday, St. Lawrence Day, August 10th, the five ships with the crews to the number of two hundred and thirty-seven set sail from the noble city of Seville…"

Pigafetta

Thus, on August 10, 1519, two years and some months after being granted his petition by King Charles I, Magellan departed from Seville with five ships: the two larger vessels *Trinidad* and *San Antonio*, and the three smaller caravels *Concepción*, *Victoria*, and *Santiago*. They were older ships and not of the quality Magellan had hoped for, but they were what he was able to obtain in the face of widespread opposition to his mission among the Spanish maritime community. In Seville, he left behind a young wife, Beatriz Barbosa, the daughter of a Portuguese friend whom he had married not long after arriving in Seville in 1517. He also left behind his recently born son Rodrigo. Magellan would never see Beatriz or Rodrigo again, and all three of them would be dead within five years.

From Seville, they sailed down the Guadalquivir River to its mouth, where they anchored at the port of Sanlúcar de Barrameda. It is from here, the same port Columbus departed from on his third voyage, that the five ships finally set out across the Atlantic about five weeks later, on September 20, 1519.

The first port of call was Tenerife, in the Canary Islands, an archipelago controlled by Spain for over a century. This first stretch of the journey was calm, but they met with severe storms after heading southwest from the Canaries and across the equator. Pigafetta, a clearly religious man, detailed some of the scares the crew had, writing:

"During these storms the body of St. Anselm appeared to us several times. And among others on a night which was very dark, at a time of bad weather, the said saint appeared in the form of a lighted torch at the height of the maintop, and remained there more than two hours and a half, to the comfort of us all. For we were in tears, expecting only the hour of death."

He documented this "supernatural" phenomenon during other parts of the trip as well:

"Here good St. Anseline met the ships; in the fancy of the mariners of the time, this airy saint appeared to favored ships in the night, and fair weather always followed the saintly apparition. He came in a robe of fire, and stood and shone on the top of the high masts or on the spars. The sailors hailed him with joy, as one sent from Heaven. Happy was the ship on the tropic sea upon whose rigging the form of good St. Anseline appeared in the night, and especially in the night of cloud and storm!

To the joy of all the ships good St. Anseline came down one night to the fleet of Magellan. The poetical Italian tells the story in this way:

"During these storms, the body of St. Anseline appeared to us several times.

One night among others he came when it was very dark on account of bad weather. He came in the form of a fire lighted at the summit of the main mast, and remained there near two hours and a half.

This comforted us greatly, for we were in tears, looking for the hour when we should perish.

When the holy light was going away from us it shed forth so great a brilliancy in our eyes that we were like people blinded for near a quarter of an hour. We called out for mercy.

Nobody expected to escape from the storm.

It is to be noted that all and as many times as the light which represents St. Anseline shows itself upon a vessel which is in a storm at sea, that vessel never is lost.

As soon as this light had departed the sea grew calmer and the wings of diverse kinds of birds appeared."

Clearly, the men were not familiar with "St. Elmo's Fire", the visible electrical discharge that often appears on the tall masts of ships during thunderstorms.

Weather wasn't the only thing giving Magellan's expedition difficulty early on. For a time, they were pursued by a fleet sent by King Manuel of Portugal, but as an initial testament to Magellan's navigational skill, the Spanish fleet successfully eluded its foes and set out for Brazil, stopping briefly in the Cape Verde islands. They were taking a risk by charting a course toward the Brazilian coast, since Brazil had already been claimed by Portugal almost 20 years earlier, and the Treaty of Tordesillas seemed to justify that claim. The Portuguese had not established much in the way of a settlement there, occupied as they were with their new Asian acquisitions in the Indian Ocean, but a violation of the agreement with his former employer Portugal could put Magellan's future claims at risk.

The fleet reached the South American coast by late November, passing by Cape St. Augustine and Cabo Frío along the Brazilian coast and heading further south to avoid lands already charted by previous Portuguese explorers. They ended up laying anchor in the bay of Río de Janeiro, not yet the major Portuguese settlement it would become.

At this point, Magellan had reached a turning point in his journey. He and Rui Faleiro had assured the Spanish crown that they would find a strait in the South American terra firma through which they could pass to what was then called the "South Sea" (the Pacific Ocean) and then to the East Indies. But the coast south from Brazil had not been accurately charted yet, so Magellan could not be genuinely certain that he would find such a passage. Furthermore, this uncertainty seems to have created an upswell of tension between him and the fellow officers and crew, no doubt exacerbated by the Spanish-Portuguese rivalries that had beset them even before they set sail.

The tensions came to a head as they sailed further to the South. After departing from Río de Janeiro, their next stop was in the Río de la Plata estuary. The expedition now stopped to replenish supplies and determine their next course of action, and the layover gave the crew time to familiarize themselves with some of the exotic surroundings. It was here that the crew met some cannibals for the first time, whom Pigafetta described as "giants" that were so tall the men of Magellan's crew were only as tall as their waists. Pigafetta explained, "They do not eat up the whole body of a man whom they take prisoner; they eat him bit by bit, and for fear that he should be spoiled, they cut him up into pieces, which they set to dry before the chimney. They eat this day by day, so as to keep in mind the memory of their enemy."

Pigafetta wasn't the only one fascinated by them; Magellan ordered that two of them be taken captive. According to Pigafetta, the crew tricked 4 of them into coming onboard and distracted them with trinkets. "Forthwith the captain had the fetters put on the feet of both of them. And when they saw the bolt across the fetters being struck with a hammer to rivet it and prevent them from being opened, these giants were afraid. But the captain made signs to them that they should suspect nothing. Nevertheless, perceiving the trick that had been played on them, they began to blow and foam at the mouth like bulls, loudly calling on Setebos (that is, the great devil) to help them."

The two others had their hands put in irons, but Magellan apparently decided to free them. Pigafetta continued, "The hands of the other two giants were bound, but it was with great difficulty; then the Captain sent them back on shore, with nine of his men to conduct them, and to bring the wife of one of those who had remained in irons, because he regretted her greatly."

As that incident suggests, the contact between Magellan's men and these "giants" was not friendly, and it soon devolved into combat. It was during this time that the expedition lost its first man after one of the crew was hit by a poisoned arrow and died shortly after. Somewhat fittingly, as Magellan's men were stopped here, Cortés was in the beginning stages of his conquest of the Aztec empire.

The Río de la Plata estuary appeared to be exactly the kind of massive portal into the South American continent that Magellan reasonably assumed to be the broad strait that would carry them across to the South Sea. However, once they sailed up the river, it was not difficult to determine that the great waters flowing southeast were in fact freshwater, meaning they could not possibly originate in an ocean on the other side of the continent. Recognizing his mistake, Magellan directed the fleet further south to what is now the Port of San Julián in Argentina, where they came to a stop in the days before Easter 1520. Magellan also made plans to spend the rest of the winter months there and set sail again in August.

It was in San Julián that a mutiny erupted against Magellan's authority, led by two Spanish captains who had always resented serving under Portuguese command. Magellan apparently managed to keep much of the crew on his side, however, and the mutinous sailors found themselves isolated and outflanked. Pigafetta described the conspiracy and its results:

"[A]s soon as we entered the port, the masters of the other four ships conspired against the captain-general to bring about his death. Whose names were Juan de Cartagena, overseer of the fleet, the treasurer Luis de Mendoza, the overseer Antonio de Coca, and Gaspar Quesada. But the treachery was discovered, because the treasurer was killed by dagger blows, then quartered. This Gaspar Quesada had his head cut off, and then he was quartered. And the overseer Juan de Cartagena, who several days later tried to commit treachery, was banished with a priest, and put in exile on that land named Patagoni."

Magellan's leadership abilities had now been thoroughly tested, but he had come out of the trial with the loyalty of his crew intact. In the weeks that followed, the resolve of the mission's participants would continue to be tested. In a reconnaissance mission to the South, the *Santiago* was wrecked near the mouth of the Santa Cruz River in what is now Southern Argentina. Of the 37 crewmen, one died and the rest were rescued, but the expedition was now down to 4 ships.

In addition to the loss of the *Santiago*, the Santa Cruz River itself was another disappointment; a brief survey demonstrated that it was clearly not the strait the expedition was seeking. After rescuing the castaways from the *Santiago*, the four remaining ships continued south along the South American coast, reaching Cape Vírgenes, which juts dramatically out to the East just above a strait separating the South American mainland from the large island of the Tierra del Fuego. This was the strait they were looking for, and the one that would later be named the Strait of Magellan, though Pigafetta's comments suggest someone else may have discovered it before them. "But the captain-general said that there was another strait which led out, saying that he knew it well and had seen it in a marine chart of the King of Portugal, which a great pilot and sailor named Martin of Bohemia had made."

Either way, an expedition sent to explore the waterway was able to confirm that the saltwater did not give way to freshwater as they proceeded inland. However, since the strait had a southeast and a southwest channel, Magellan had the *Concepcion* and the *Santo Antonio* explore the southeast while the *Trinidad* and *Victoria* went southwest. During this exploration, the *Santo Antonio* became separated from the *Concepcion*, and its men decided to mutiny. With that, the *Santo Antonio* turned around to head back to Spain without informing the other ships.

The reduced fleet of three ships set off westward along the strait on November 1, 1520. Because of this date, the original name given the waterway was the *Estrecho de Todos los Santos* or Strait of All Saints; only after Magellan's death would it become the *Estrecho de Magallanes*. By the end of the month, they had reached the South Sea, which Magellan, impressed by the initial stillness of the waters they encountered on the other end of the strait, renamed the *Mar Pacífico* or Pacific Ocean. By some accounts, the Portuguese captain wept upon first passing through the western end of the strait into the sea. Although Vasco Núñez de Balboa had reached the Pacific traveling westward by land across Panama some seven years earlier, Magellan's crew were the first Europeans to reach the great ocean travelling westward by sea, an accomplishment that had been sought for decades by Columbus and many after him. Successfully sailing through the previously uncharted strait, which cuts a tortuous path along the Tierra del Fuego and then through an intricate archipelago to the west of it, was undoubtedly one of the more impressive feats among the many performed by European mariners in the Age of Exploration.

Despite the triumph of Magellan's enterprise in achieving its basic goal, many more challenges were to follow. The most fundamental was that the crew had run desperately low on supplies because the anticipated passage had required a much greater southern detour than had been projected by Magellan and Faleiro before setting out. While they might have tarried somewhere along the South American coast to gather what food supplies and fresh water they could, such a stop would entail risks, particularly because the territories were at that point totally unknown and uncharted by Europeans. An encounter with hostile indigenous groups could even further reduce the already diminished crew, and going ashore under uncertain conditions risked a repetition of the kind of shipwreck that had befallen the *Santiago* on the other side of the South American continent. Thus, pressed on by the strong Humboldt or Peru current that runs northward along the western shores of South America, the fleet continued onwards, first some leagues to the north up the coast of what is now Chile. Then, around the middle of December, they headed back out into open ocean, not knowing when they would reach land again.

Had Magellan's crew known the expanse of the Pacific Ocean, it's safe to say they would not have sailed west. It would be more than 3 months before they would see land again, and they had nowhere near enough supplies for such a journey. Pigafetta described just how dire their straits became. "We only ate old biscuit reduced to powder, and full of grubs, and we drank water that had turned yellow and smelled." When that failed, the crew started eating "ox hides that were under the main yard." Rats were eventually consumed, and some even took to eating leather, cloth, sawdust, and anything else they could scrounge from the ship.

Not surprisingly, many of the sailors onboard came down with scurvy and other diseases. The gums of some men swelled so much that they simply could not eat at all. Pigafetta passed some of his time trying to learn the language of one of the captive "giants", at least until that giant died. Both of the captives died during this part of the trip, as did nearly 30 of the crew. Another 30 were on the verge of death before they would see meaningful land.

Not surprisingly, morale reached a desperate level. Although Magellan's leadership was apparently effective at keeping many of the men on the crew loyal, mutiny was probably only avoided because everyone on the ships knew that turning back to Spain would at this point be a longer journey than reaching the intended destination of the Spice Islands, and that they would be unlikely to survive such an effort.

Around the end of January, several small islands were sighted, somewhere in what is now French Polynesia, but they were inhabited only by birds. It was not until over a month later that they arrived, and laid anchor, at the island of Guam in the Mariana Islands on March 6, 1521, which they nicknamed "Island of Thieves" because some of the natives came onboard and stole whatever they could get their hands on. Nevertheless, Magellan's crew was certainly more than happy to be there, and they were able to obtain food and supplies for the first time in over three months before continuing their journey. Guam would later be successively conquered by Spain, the United States, and Japan, as it was regarded by all three powers as a crucial eastern gateway to the Pacific, but Magellan and his fleet did not remain for long, and Spain would not actually establish control over the island for another century or so.

Magellan's communications with the King of Spain suggest that he was oriented well enough to know how to reach the Spice Islands from Guam and the Marianas, but he chose to direct the fleet southwest toward the islands that would later become known as the Philippines. Less than two weeks after its landing in Guam, the Spanish flotilla had reached the island of Homonhon. It seems that Magellan was eager to make friendly contact with natives in this group of islands to assure he had a place to establish a safe haven in case of any hostile encounters with the Portuguese in the Spice Islands. The Philippines had apparently been visited by Portuguese sailors already at this point, but they had not yet been brought into the Portuguese sphere of influence in the East.

The diplomatic efforts in the Philippines initially bore fruit for Magellan, thanks in part to the translation efforts of his longtime Malay slave and companion Enrique. Through an exchange of gifts, he was able to forge an alliance with the chieftain of Limasawa Island, who then directed him to the larger island of Cebu nearby. Pigafetta described their contact with the natives:

"That people became very familiar and friendly, and explained many things in their language, and told the names of some islands which they beheld. The island where they dwelt was called Zuluam, and it was not large. As they were sufficiently agreeable and conversible the crews had great pleasure with them. The Captain seeing that they were of this good spirit, conducted them to the ship and showed them specimens of all his goods—that he most desired—cloves, cinnamon, pepper, ginger, nutmeg, mace, and gold.

He also had shots fired with his artillery, at which they were so much afraid that they wished to jump from the ship into the sea. They made signs that the things which the

Captain had shown them grew there.

When they wished to go they took leave of the Captain and of the crew with very good manners and gracefulness, promising to come back.

Friday, the 22d of March, the above-mentioned people, who had promised to return, came about midday with two boats laden with the said fruit, cochi, sweet oranges, a vessel of palm wine, and a cock, to give us to understand that they had poultry in their country.

The lord of these people was old, and had his face painted, and had gold rings suspended to his ears, which they name 'schione,' and the others had many bracelets and rings of gold on their arms, with a wrapper of linen round their head. We remained at this place eight days; the Captain went there every day to see his sick men, whom he had placed on this island to refresh them; and he gave them himself every day the water of this said fruit, the cocho, which comforted them much."

Location of the Philippines

However, this alliance set off the fateful chain of events that would deprive Magellan of achieving his final goal of reaching the Spice Islands. Magellan had been directed to go to Cebu, but he was still a little weary about the kind of greeting his crew would receive there. Pigafetta explains how Magellan ensured they would be safe upon their arrival: "On Sunday the seventh of April, about noon, we entered the port of Zzubu, having passed by many villages, where we saw some houses which were built on trees. And nearing the principal town the captain-general ordered all the ships to put out their flags. Then we lowered the sails as is done when one is about to fight, and fired all the artillery, at which the people of those places were in great fear."

As it turned out, the artillery barrage was unnecessary because the alliance with Limasawa ensured the sailors were greeted hospitably in Cebu, where the chieftain, Rajah Humabon, and his consort and top advisors all accepted baptism as Christians. Pigafetta described the conversion of the natives. "And the captain told them that they should not become Christians for fear of us, or in order to please us, but that if they wished to become Christians, it should be with a good heart and for the love of God. For that, if they did not become Christians, we should show them no displeasure. But that those who became Christians would be more regarded and better treated than the others. Then all cried out together with one voice that they wished to become Christians not for fear, nor to please us, but of their own free will. Then the captain said that if they became Christians he would leave them weapons which Christians use..."

Based on their contact, Magellan apparently mistakenly believed Rajah Humabon to be king over all of the neighboring islands, and therefore believed he had secured the loyalty of the remaining population of the archipelago. In fact, the local politics were far more complicated; local chieftains operated in varying degrees of alliance with one another, and there was no particular one who had power over the others. It may have been this mistake that sealed Magellan's fate when he proceeded to the island of Mactan, where he hoped the ruler would also accept Christianity, perhaps believing him to be subordinate to Humabon. It has also been widely speculated that Rajah Humabon had a score to settle with Mactan's chieftain, Lapu Lapu, and manipulated Magellan by sending him to Mactan. According to this viewpoint, Humabon expected hostilities to ensue between Lapu Lapu and Magellan's crew in the hope that the Europeans' firepower would propel them to victory over his rival.

Whatever the case may be, Lapu Lapu refused to submit to Magellan and did not accept the offer of baptism. In general, this kind of supposed "insubordination" was regarded among conquistadors as sufficient justification for waging war, and in this instance Magellan also hoped that subduing Mactan would strengthen his alliance with Cebu, which he believed to be the superior kingdom. It is also believed that Humabon assured Magellan that he would not need a large force to subdue Lapu Lapu.

On April 27, 1521, a force of about 60 men, including crewmen and an uncertain number of native allies from Cebu headed toward Mactan, armed and ready to fight the inhabitants. As it turned out, Magellan was leading his men ashore against upwards of 1,500-3,000 warriors under Lapu Lapu's command. On other occasions during their era of global conquest, Spanish forces were able to eke out victory despite comparable odds out of a mixture of audacity, spectacular firepower, and sheer brutality and ruthlessness, but the coral reefs surrounding Mactan foiled the initial strategy of assaulting the enemy warriors with the cannons on board ship. Instead, they were forced to anchor the ships far from shore and make their way ashore swimming and wading, all the while being pelted by thousands of arrows and spears.

The crew were certainly equipped with better weapons, but their muskets and crossbows were awkward, inaccurate, and slow to reload, which made it hard for them to inflict casualties on the more mobile combatants on shore. Magellan sent some Spaniards to set fire to some of the thatched structures near the shore, in the hope of creating confusion and fear, but apparently this only heightened the resolve of Lapu Lapu and his men, who quickly killed the arsonists.

Pigafetta was present and described the attack, explaining how Magellan's men were forced to conduct their fight while still wading in the water off shore. "Our large pieces of artillery which were in the ships could not help us, because they were firing at too long range, so that we continued to retreat for more than a good crossbow flight from the shore, still fighting, and in water up to our knees. And they followed us, hurling poisoned arrows four or six times; while, recognizing the captain, they turned toward him inasmuch they hurled arrows very close to his head."

Pigafetta described the chaotic climax of the failed assault:

So many of them charged down upon us that they shot the captain through the right leg with a poisoned arrow. On that account, he ordered us to retire slowly, but the men took to flight, except six or eight of us who remained with the captain. The natives shot only at our legs, for the latter were bare; and so many were the spears and stones that they hurled at us, that we could offer no resistance. The mortars in the boats could not aid us as they were too far away. So we continued to retire for more than a good crossbow flight from the shore always fighting up to our knees in the water. The natives continued to pursue us, and picking up the same spear four or six times, hurled it at us again and again. Recognizing the captain, so many turned upon him that they knocked his helmet off his head twice, but he always stood firmly like a good knight, together with some others. Thus did we fight for more than one hour, refusing to retire farther. An Indian hurled a bamboo spear into the captain's face, but the latter immediately killed him with his lance, which he left in the Indian's body. Then, trying to lay hand on sword, he could draw it out but halfway, because he had been wounded in the arm with a bamboo spear. When the natives saw that, they all hurled themselves upon him. One of them wounded him on the left leg with a large cutlass, which resembles a scimitar, only being larger. That caused the captain to fall face downward, when immediately they rushed upon him with iron and bamboo spears and with their cutlasses, until they killed our mirror, our light, our comfort, and our true guide. When they wounded him, he turned back many times to see whether we were all in the boats. Thereupon, beholding him dead, we, wounded, retreated, as best we could, to the boats, which were already pulling off."

Upon Magellan's death, the remaining Spaniards turned back and retreated toward the ships. Shocked, disoriented, and outnumbered, the remaining forces that had stayed on board the ship retreated to Cebu, leaving Magellan's body behind. Centuries later, the victorious Lapu Lapu was proclaimed a national hero in the Philippines as the first to successfully drive off imperialist invaders from the nation's shores.

After this disaster, only 120 of the original crew were still alive, and the expedition had lost its leader, leaving the fleet and its crew in disarray. Making matters worse, Humabon ended up reconsidering his alliance with the Europeans for reasons that are not entirely clear. He may have simply felt that they had ceded any advantage they might have had for his own power by failing to defeat Lapu Lapu, but he also may also have plotted against them with Enrique, Magellan's interpreter. Magellan had declared in his will that Enrique should be freed from servitude upon his death, but Magellan's successor, Juan Sebastián Elcano, refused to do so. Back in Cebu, about thirty of the Spaniards were poisoned at Humabon's command during a large feast to which they had been invited, and at this point Enrique managed to escape with help from Humabon.

Elcano

Realizing the danger, the remaining members of the crew now needed to flee, as they might easily be massacred by a much larger native force. Without enough men to command all three ships, so the *Concepción* was taken out to sea and burned, and the two remaining ships sailed onward to the Spice Islands, where they made several trading stops on Brunei (which Pigafetta described as "a collection of houses built on piles over the water, where were twenty-five thousand fires or families") and other islands. Maximilianus Transylvanus described their stop here after interviewing survivors from the *Victoria*:

"They came to the shores of the Island of Solo, where they heard that there were pearls as big as dove's eggs, and sometimes as hen's eggs, but which can only be fished up from the very deepest sea. Our men brought no large pearl, because the season of the year did not allow of the fishery. But they testify that they had taken an oyster in that region, the flesh of which weighed forty-seven pounds. For which reason I could easily believe that pearls of that great size are found there; for it is clearly proved that pearls are the product of shellfish. And to omit nothing, our men constantly affirm that the islanders of Porne told him that the King wore in his crown two pearls of the size of a goose's egg.

Hence they went to the Island of Gilo, where they saw men with ears so long and pendulous that they reached to their shoulders. When our men were mightily astonished at this, they learnt from the natives that there was another island not far off where the men had ears not only pendulous, but so long and broad that one of them would cover the whole head if they wanted it (cum exusu esset). But our men, who sought not monsters but spices, neglecting this nonsense, went straight to the Moluccas, and they discovered them eight months after their Admiral, Magellan, had fallen in Matan. The islands are five in number, and are called Tarante, Muthil, Thidore, Mare, and Matthien; some on this side some on the other, and some upon the equinoctial line.

One produces cloves, another nutmegs, and another cinnamon. All are near to each other, but small and rather narrow."

Magellan's expedition had successfully reached the Spice Islands by sailing west, albeit with considerably more difficulty than anticipated. But now there was disagreement about how to return to Spain, and the remaining two ships parted ways, with the *Trinidad* attempting to sail back across the Pacific and the *Victoria* taking the risk of traveling the Portuguese route around the Cape of Good Hope. Strangely enough, it would be the *Trinidad* that was halted by Portuguese officials, even as it sailed away from territories most closely held by Portugal, and its captain and crew arrested.

Meanwhile, the *Victoria*, under the command of Elcano, sailed across the Indian Ocean and around Africa. On May 19, 1522, the *Victoria* passed by the Cape of Good Hope, but by now the crew was starving and their ship was literally falling apart. Their plight was so desperate that when they reached the Portuguese-held Cape Verde islands on July 9, 1522, some of the men went ashore to try to obtain supplies. Suspicious, the Portuguese detained 13 of them, leaving the *Victoria* to make a speedy exit.

On September 6, 1522, the *Victoria* arrived back in Seville, Spain. One of the most intriguing anecdotes about their return was that they discovered they had lost a day because they had sailed west while the Earth rotated the other way, so despite keeping an accurate daily log, their date was still inaccurate. This would lead to the creation of an International Date Line.

Though the ship was laden with valuable spices, when the *Victoria* pulled into port she was manned by a desperate and starving crew. The survivors onboard the *Victoria* had traveled nearly 38,000 miles, and of the 237 that had set sail with Magellan in August 1519, only 18 had made it back to the original port from which they had set sail over 3 years earlier. 4 of the 55 men who had been arrested onboard the *Trinidad* made it back to Spain in 1525 (the other 51 having died from disease or battle). More than 90% of the men who sailed with Magellan fell victim to the voyage, as did the captain himself.

The *Victoria* was the only of the five ships that succeeded in circumnavigating the globe, and so it was that Elcano rather than Magellan was awarded with a medal by Charles I in honor of this achievement. Although the trip had ended catastrophically for Magellan and the vast majority of his crew, it had essentially achieved what he had proposed. It would take some decades for the Spanish colonization of the Philippines to succeed in earnest, but the reconnaissance achieved by the mission had laid the groundwork for that enterprise and for the lucrative trade routes across the Pacific that would be developed over the next century. Its main achievement was to forge a vital link between two processes of imperial expansion and commercial expansion that until then had proceeded separately: the Spanish colonization of the American continent and the Portuguese incursions into the Indian Ocean.

Furthermore, until the construction of the Panama Canal in the early twentieth century, the Strait of Magellan would remain the principal sea route between the Atlantic and Pacific, and the challenge of its navigation would be taken up by many generations of later sailors. Magellan and the diverse crew that accompanied him suffered and died en masse, but they became some of the earliest pioneers of the age of globalization.

Chapter 12: Pizarro's Conquest of the Incas

Pizarro's First Two Expeditions and the Capitulación

Despite his modest success in the new colony, Pizarro clearly had his eyes on a bigger prize, and this fact is not terribly surprising: Panama was in a backwater area that had not yielded the wealth in gold and other precious items that had been anticipated. And while the Pacific had been reached, Asia was still a long way away.

On the other hand, the Spaniards now had reliable informants among the local natives, and it was from them that they heard rumors of a great kingdom to the South, named Virú or Birú, a place of fabulous wealth and abundance. In the meantime, by the early 1520s the settlers of Panama had heard news of Cortés's conquest to the north, a development that certainly raised their hopes and likely inspired their envy. Perhaps most importantly, there was now a propitious environment for an adventurous man to raise up an expedition, men eager to take part, and financiers willing to cover the costs of equipping several ships and several hundred men with the necessary supplies and weapons for a trip of uncertain duration and results. In Diego de Almagro, another Spaniard of humble origins settled in Panama, Pizarro found a partner and collaborator. The two signed a contract on a joint venture to the south in 1524 and promised to divide all eventual proceeds between them. The relationship with Almagro would be a crucial one for the rest of Pizarro's life, and would end up being a pivotal factor in his death.

By the time Pizarro and Almagro began preparing their first venture down the Pacific coast, they had been preceded by Pascal de Anadagoya, an explorer of Basque origin. Andagoya's 1522 excursion had failed as a mission of conquest because of hostility from the natives on the coast and poor weather, but his returning crew had brought back persuasive evidence of the existence of a great and wealthy empire to the south. It was now only a matter of time before other would-be conquistadors took up the challenge, so Pizarro and Almagro hurriedly assembled a small expeditionary force of about 80,and managed to obtain permission from Dávila, to whom they and any lands they managed to conquer would remain subordinate.

Pizarro set out late in September 1524, while Almagro stayed behind with the intention of recruiting more men and catching up with the forward party. As it turned out, the mission was for the most part a disaster. Like Andagoya and his men before them, the Spaniards under Pizarro's command were met with relentless hostility from the natives on the shore, and poor weather and limited supplies made things even worse. In the end, the entire force returned in early 1525 with little to show for their efforts.

What they had seen, though, evidently confirmed the rich rewards of conquest if it was achieved, and so they set out again in August of 1526, this time with a force about twice as large as the first expedition's. As in their own previous expedition and Andagoya's, they met with hostility all along the coast of what are now Colombia and Ecuador, and their attempts to establish footholds on the land and explore the interior bore little fruit. The conditions were so poor and the palpable rewards so scarce that by 1527, many of the men preferred to return to Panama, where they went with Almagro when he returned to gather supplies and recruit replacements.

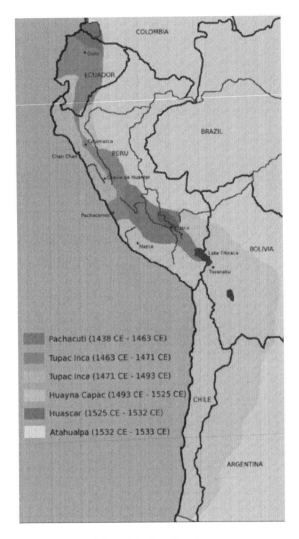

Map of the Inca Empire

Meanwhile, Pizarro and a small group pressed on, and the results were finally encouraging. They reached Tumbes, a coastal city at the edge of the Incan domains. They were impressed with the more "civilized" appearance of the settlement and with the great quantities of gold and silver belonging to the local *cacique*, a tributary of the Incas, and they were generally treated in a friendly way by the inhabitants. One of them, a young boy, accepted baptism and later returned with Pizarro to Panama. Felipillo, as he came to be called by the Spaniards, would become their principal translator in their engagements with the Inca emperor and his emissaries in future years.

On the strength of the solid evidence of wealth that he brought back from Tumbes, Pizarro returned to Spain in 1528 – he had not been back in 20 years – to seek permission from the crown to undertake the conquest of Peru. This way, he would be able to operate independently rather than under the command of the governor of Panama, and even more importantly he would have access to a larger share of all proceeds. Probably encouraged by the recent success of Cortés and himself desperate for new sources of revenue, Charles V was receptive to Pizarro's solicitation and in the end granted him the licence or *capitulación* necessary to undertake the conquest. On the strength of this political coup and his promises of great wealth, Pizarro was able to recruit a large force of men from his native Extremadura, including his four half-brothers. Back in Panama, meanwhile, Almagro was assembling more participants, while the priest Hernando de Luque, a third partner, gathered funds from investors.

While the capitulación was probably Pizarro's most impressive accomplishment thus far, it had the side effect of creating tension between him and Almagro, a tension that would continue to build and have a decisive influence on both men's fates. Upon Pizarro's return to Panama, Almagro was unhappy with what seemed to him the unfair and unequal division of the rewards of conquest determined by the king. Pizarro was to be Governor and Captain General of Peru (the same position won by Cortés in Mexico), while Almagro obtained the far less glorious concession of the governorship of Tumbes. Furthermore, the presence of a large contingent of Pizarro's family appeared to Almagro an affront to their supposed partnership, since he rightly surmised that Pizarro would be inclined to hand out lucrative rewards to his brothers. While the nascent conflict did not derail the preparations in any serious ways, Almagro's resentments would now be left to simmer beneath the surface, and it would only be a matter of time before they would explode.

The Inca Empire

According to history as created by Inca oral tradition, preserved by memory keepers and written down by Spanish commentators after the conquest, there was no culture or civilization in Peru before the Incas arrived on the scene. Given these origins, anthropologists speculate that in the interest of ensuring their dominance in the area, the Incas purposely extinguished any local histories that existed in their empire, so that for all the peoples of the empire history began when the Incas appeared. Ironically, this was accomplished in much the same way and with similar results as the Spanish attempt to destroy the Incas' own memory of their history and civilization.

The Inca referred to their own empire as *Tawantinsuyu*, which meant "four parts together" in their language. This is because the Inca Empire was administered as four provincial departments: Chinchasuyu (NW), Antiwuyu (NE), Kuntisuyu (SW), and Qullasuyu (SE). These *Tawantinsuyu* or four regions or the four united provinces were connected to Cuzco by roads along which runners could pass quickly to deliver information from the court of the ruler to provincial governors and vice versa. The roads also allowed the quick movement of warriors to any part of the empire where they were needed, and it accommodated the large parties of those rendering mit'a or labor to make their way to construction sites, which were especially numerous in the last years of the empire.

The extent of the Inca road system is evidence of its importance in the economy and administration of the Empire. The backbone of the system of communication was the Qhapaq Ñan, which ran 3,700 miles along the length of the Andes, connecting Santiago to Quito. Many other roads allowed for the quick negotiation of the often very mountainous terrain of the empire, which encompassed a large part of western South America from southern Ecuador and Columbia and western Bolivia to northwest Argentina, and central Chile. It is estimated that the network of Inca roads totaled some 24,000 miles. With that said, the use of the word "road" is a bit of a misnomer, because the Inca had no wheeled vehicles and no pack animals. Since they always moved on foot, certain stretches of a road could more aptly be described as a narrow path.

The Imperial population connected by the road system is estimated to have been anywhere from 4 to 37 million. It is presumed that many of the quipu that have been preserved up to the present day are census records, but in the absence of a key to their code it is not possible to know with any degree of accuracy the population of the Inca Empire.

The Incas spoke a language they called runasimi, and which the conquistadors called quechua. Quechua was introduced in the Inca culture after 1338, so it is assumed that they had another language prior to settling in Cuzco. It is also believed that the elite may have continued to use this original language. Quechua, which has eight figures of speech, no articles, no gender and a small vocabulary, was imposed as the *lingua franca* by the Incas in their empire to facilitate communication between many different cultural groups that fell under Inca administration.

The group of indigenous Andeans that established themselves as the Incas at Cuzco developed a culture that was in some ways unique and in other ways similar to that of other indigenous Andean peoples. Like all good imperialists, the Inca were expert assimilationists, making it often difficult to determine with certainty what the Inca inherited from earlier cultures and what was unique to them. For example, many of the basic ideas in their building projects had reached particularly high levels of development before the Incas employed them. Vertical archipelago agriculture practiced by the Incas, in which terraced fields were layered on mountainsides, and the construction of bridges, roads and irrigation canals, were common in Andean cultures long before the rise of the Incas.

The Inca ruler, who claimed direct descent from the sun through the founder Manco Capac, considered the people of the empire his sons and all the women his spouses. His authority was spread throughout the empire by his court of elite nobles who received their power by direct connection to the ruler through royal blood.

The Inca developed a sophisticated system of imperial administration that is not yet completely understood. In the conquered territories, they apparently used the heads of the leading local families as administrators. These chiefs were called *curaca* under the Incas, and the office was hereditary. At the same time, these local administrators were not to call themselves Incas and were clearly kept in a subservient position to the elite of Cuzco. The *curaca* were responsible for ensuring that appropriate tribute was forwarded to the Inca Emperor, mainly in the form of mit'a or labor. To ensure that Imperial authority remained consistent, the children of the *curaca* were sent to Cuzco to be taught Inca administrative systems.

Not much is known about the Inca system of law and its application to the conquered territories. Presumably there were local courts that enforced edicts from Cuzco and ensured that surpluses in agricultural produce were stored and forwarded to the elite when demanded.

Pizarro, accompanied by his brothers and the translator Felipillo, set out for Peru from Panama in December 1530 with a force of nearly two hundred men. Almagro remained behind, recruiting and gathering supplies, with a plan to join the initial force in a few months. Having arrived on the coast of what is now Ecuador, they made their way by land to Tumbes, where they were surprised to find the city sacked and partly abandoned. From those local inhabitants they could find they gleaned important intelligence: the great Inca empire was immersed in a civil war. The emperor Huayna Capac had died suddenly, most likely of smallpox, which had made its way from the Spanish settlements of Central America down the trade routes running down the ridge of the Andes and was now decimating the Peruvian population before any Spaniards had even arrived. Although many Spaniards had died of tropical diseases in the Indies, the effect of new viruses on the indigenous population had been devastating, and smallpox and measles had already helped Cortés decisively in Mexico. After Huayna Capac's death, two of his sons, Huascar and Atahualpa, had both claimed the throne, and each had raised up a sizable enough army to defend the claim. Whereas Cortés had taken advantage of the resentments of tributary tribes toward their Aztec overlords, Pizarro was now able to use the divisions within the Inca state to his own advantage.

The Fall of the Inca

The Inca Empire may have consisted of 4 parts, but the unity was quite fragile, as the empire had only existed in its current state for about a century when Pizarro arrived. Brought together by a combination of military conquests and peaceful takeovers involving royal intermarriage, a combination of tribute, trade, and centralized administration held the various territories under Inca rule together, even as they remained politically and culturally relatively autonomous. Still, the first Spaniards to see Peru commented on the orderliness of their system of government and the impressive productivity of their agriculture, which produced grain surpluses stored in a network of warehouses and distributed during drought years. With some more recalcitrant conquered groups, the rulers had undertaken forced resettlements and practical enslavement, but for the most part, Inca rule had been peaceful and prosperous for some time. The war between Huascar and Atahualpa had introduced a disorienting period of political chaos and conflicted loyalties that would be initially exploited and then seriously exacerbated by the newly arrived Spaniards.

After months of gathering the latest intelligence, Pizarro determined that Atahualpa had gained a decisive advantage in the conflict and that his troops had taken Huascar captive in the capital of Cuzco. Having been based in the north, Atahualpa was now marching south with a large army toward Cuzco. Pizarro, with fewer than 200 men, decided to go for broke against a far superior force, in the hope of striking a dramatic blow against the Incas. Probably inspired by Cortés's strategy in Mexico, which involved the capture of Moctezuma for ransom, he hatched the plan of leading Atahualpa into a trap and taking him hostage. The plans for the trap were probably also borrowed from Cortés and his lieutenant Pedro de Alvarado, who first in the city of Cholula and then in the Aztec capital of Tenochtitlán managed to ambush thousands of indigenous nobles and warriors by cornering them in confined spaces and attacking them by surprise.

The enterprise was an enormous gamble premised entirely on treachery and unprovoked violence, and even if it succeeded, there was no guarantee that it would lead to ultimate victory. Even though Almagro might show up with a larger force of several hundred, Atahualpa had perhaps as many as 10,000 in his immediate retinue and was supported by several armies of more than 30,000. The terrain was mountainous, climactically variable, and completely unknown to the Spaniards. They had few advantages other than their own unscrupulousness and the fact that their motives were entirely unknown to their enemies.

After a harsh trek up into the heights of the Andes, Pizarro and his men reached the city of Cajamarca, mostly abandoned because of the civil war. Throughout their traversal, they were watched by the Inca's spies, and given their vulnerability, it is surprising that they were not ambushed and slaughtered by their numerically superior adversaries. Instead, they established themselves in Cajamarca and sent messengers to the nearby encampment where Atahualpa was currently staying, and persuaded him to meet with Pizarro and the other Spaniards in Cajamarca. Little is known about his motives, but one can assume that, confident after his victory over his brother and unimpressed by the small ragtag band of foreigners, it simply did not occur to him that they represented a serious threat to his power.

Whatever the case, when he arrived in Cajamarca, he came with a force of about 6,000 men, accompanied by a large contingent of nobles. These men were equipped with stone-age weapons such as wooden clubs and obsidian bladed spears. In the central square of Cajamarca, Atahualpa found only a few Spaniards, which made him feel perfectly safe about leading his entire retinue in. He could not know that Pizarro's hundred or so men were concealed in some of the building surrounding the square heavily armed and ready to attack.

What occurred next has been a matter of debate among historians for some time, but the essential facts seem to be the following. Vicente de Valverde, a priest who was accompanying Pizarro's expedition, emerged into the square with the interpreter Felipillo and read out the *requerimiento*, a document that demanded submission to the authority of the Pope and the king of Spain. Failure to submit to the terms of the *requerimiento* was regarded, in the legal apparatus the Spanish government had created to justify and legitimize conquest, as sufficient grounds for waging a "just war" against a non-Christian people. Having recited this strange document to Atahualpa, Valverde placed an equally strange document in his hand: a Catholic breviary. Not only could Atahualpa of course not read it, he had never even seen a book before. Puzzled by the gesture, he peered at the object for a moment, and then dropped it on the ground. Valverde declared to the Spaniards in hiding that the heathen had rejected the true faith, which gave them *carte blanche* for an attack. A round of cannon and musket fire burst out onto the square from the surrounding buildings, and a contingent of Spaniards on horseback made their way into the assembly of Indians, hacking at them with swords. The goal was to take the Inca emperor captive, and to do this they hacked off the arms of the private guards who carried his litter. The combat spilled out onto a surrounding plain, where a larger Inca army waited but failed to turn back the course of events. Those who did not fall to the Spaniards that evening fled back to their encampment.

Incredibly, Pizarro and his small force had managed to take the emperor captive and in the process slaughtered thousands of his soldiers. In truth, the Incas would never recover from the shock and trauma inflicted by this initial blow. Atahualpa, now their hostage, was apparently still unaware of their intention of total conquest of Peru, because he could have likely orchestrated his own rescue and the destruction of the invaders by summoning an overwhelmingly large army. Instead, he agreed to pay the ransom of an entire room filled with gold and two with silver, and he sent his emissaries to gather the necessary riches. He may have hoped that once they received the ransom, they would take the plunder back home and disturb him no more. In any case, while imprisoned by the Spaniards he arranged for his brother Huascar to be executed, suggesting that he was confident he would regain his position. This execution may have been a fatal move on his part, since it alienated many of the nobles of Cuzco and the southern provinces of the empire, most of whom had supported Huascar and would now be inclined to initially (and mistakenly) regard the Spaniards as liberators.

Meanwhile, the arrival of Almagro with over a hundred men created a restlessness among the Spaniards in Cajamarca, who wished to proceed toward the capital of Cuzco in search of more booty. Once the ransom was gathered, the Spaniards hesitated about what to do. It had been partly a delaying tactic, and now Atahualpa had less value to them alive. Since they intended to conquer his entire territory, they were obviously not going to allow him to return to his throne in Cuzco. Thus, in a move that proved controversial even at the time, Pizarro ordered the emperor's execution, hypocritically claiming on trumped up charges that Atahualpa had murdered his brother, practiced idolatry and attempted to revolt against the Spanish. Pizarro condemned him first to be baptized, then strangled and incinerated. This was particularly galling to the Inca, who believed that the burning of their bodies or corpses would prevent them from entering the afterlife.

Portrait depicting the death of Atahualpa, the last Sapa Inca.

Upon hearing the news of the Inca leader's death, Charles V wrote to Pizarro: "We have been displeased by the death of Atahualpa, since he was a monarch, and particularly as it was done in the name of justice." No European monarch appreciated the precedent established by regicide, even if it took place an ocean away. Nevertheless, while the execution of Atahualpa would prove a questionable action as far as the legitimacy of the conquest was concerned for the king of Spain and others, for the moment it allowed the Spaniards to fill the leadership vacuum in Peru in a way that would be favorable to their own situation. Trying to earn the trust of the Huascar faction in Cuzco, they arranged for Huascar's brother, Tupac Hualpa, to ascend to the throne. The plan to be treated as allies and liberators in Cuzco did not ease their transit to the Inca capital. In the harsh and cold terrain between Cajamarca and Cuzco, they were repeatedly beset by armies loyal to Atahualpa, which managed to inflict significant casualties on them.

Pizarro and his ragged and exhausted army of conquistadors arrived in Cuzco in the middle of November 1533, almost a year after the massacre in Cajamarca. They were amazed by what they saw, and Pizarro reported back to the Spanish king, "This city is the greatest and the finest ever seen in this country or anywhere in the Indies... We can assure your Majesty that it is so beautiful and has such fine buildings that it would be remarkable even in Spain."

Unsurprisingly, it did not take the newcomers very long to lose whatever good will may have been directed at them by the partisans of Huascar, since they immediately set about looting gold and other valuables and treating the inhabitants with contempt and brutality. A new emperor had been appointed, Manco Inca, whom the Spaniards viewed as a puppet who would allow them to rule from behind the scenes. Manco, however, had his own agenda, and probably thought that once the Spaniards had exhausted the available riches they would move on.

Meanwhile, other conflicts emerged. Some native groups became allies of the Spanish, while others bided their time, waiting to drive out the invaders. And the northern provinces, generally loyal to Atahualpa, still needed to be brought under control. Almagro and Sebastián de Benalcázar set out to do just that, but once they had arrived in the region of Quito, they found themselves facing off with another Spaniard, Cortés's former lieutenant Pedro de Alvarado, who had set out on his own conquest mission from the northern Colombian coast. A battle nearly erupted between the two Spanish armies, but in the end Alvarado was successfully bribed with a share of Atahualpa's ransom.

By now, however, a second and more deadly intra-Spanish conflict was afoot. Almagro, who had arrived late to Cajamarca, felt marginalized by the power of Pizarro and his brothers, particularly since he had never received a share of Atahualpa's ransom. He and his men believed that they had not yet enjoyed the promised fruits of conquest, even though their support had been crucial in the march to Cuzco. Through slow communication with Spain, it was established that the king had granted Pizarro jurisdiction over the north of the Inca empire and Almagro control over the south. It was unclear, though, which of them would obtain control over the all-important city of Cuzco, since the city lay at the dead center of Inca territory (its name translates as "the navel").

The attempts to defray the conflict probably exacerbated it. Judging that Cuzco was too far inland to serve as the Spanish capital, Pizarro founded and settled in the new city of Lima on a stretch of coast under his own control, which would assure his own importance and give him easier access to supplies and reinforcements from Panama. Meanwhile, Almagro set out on an expedition to conquer the territories to the south, obviously hoping to find territories even wealthier than the Inca heartland. He and his men were not prepared for the arid wasteland of the Atacama Desert that stretches between Peru and what is now Chile, and their two-year expedition brought much suffering and death to the Spaniards themselves and the natives they met, with no new wealth to show for it.

An Incomplete Conquest

While the *almagristas*, as they were called, struggled across the Atacama, Pizarro put two of his younger brothers in charge of Cuzco so as to ensconce himself firmly in Lima. Gonzalo and Juan Pizarro were, unsurprisingly, disastrous governors who essentially gave free rein to the Spaniards to plunder, enslave, and rape. The alliances forged on the basis of the execution of Atahualpa were soon dissolved, and the young emperor Manco now decided to take matters into his own hands. The invaders in Cuzco still only numbered about 200, and they seemed distracted enough by their pillage to appear. Manco raised up an army of thousands, and in 1536 his forces laid siege to both Cuzco and Lima. Pizarro sent a desperate request for reinforcements from Panama, but the decisive support came in the form of the Almagro party, which arrived back in Cuzco in the Spring of 1537 and successfully drove away Manco and the Inca army.

While this sounds at first blush like a reversal of the tensions between Almagro and Pizarro, it was anything but. This was not a gesture of Spanish unity, it was an act of conquest. Almagro and his men took control of Cuzco, which they believed was theirs by right, and took the Pizarro brothers prisoner.

Meanwhile, the war with Manco was still not over. The Inca emperor had been driven away but not defeated, and he would return to give the Spaniards trouble for some years to come. But the central conflict that now consumed Peru was the one between Pizarro and Almagro, a conflict whose origins began before Pizarro's conquest of the Incas had even begun.

Almagro, embittered and furious, was determined to keep Cuzco, and in order to establish his claim he set out to Lima to take on his former business partner. Meanwhile, more Spaniards were arriving from Panama and beyond, desperate to get their hands on some of the land's abundant gold. The new colony was on the verge of descending into chaos, and Pizarro was determined to establish a persuasive and lasting hold on power. This made him reluctant to negotiate with Almagro, especially after the affront of the latter's arrest of his brothers in Cuzco. A series of battles between supporters of Pizarro and Almagro followed, even as Manco began to gather forces for a new attack.

Pizarro's most military capable brother, Hernando, finally defeated Almagro and his followers at Las Salinas in April of 1538, after which he dragged Almagro back to Cuzco. Almagro was tried, imprisoned, and ultimately garrotted in prison. His body was displayed in Cuzco's central square as a warning to his followers.

If the killing of Atahualpa was controversial, the execution of Almagro was even more so. While it removed the leader of resistance against Pizarro's power, it strengthened the resolve against Pizarro. It was also regarded as a treacherous and criminal power grab when word of the latest developments arrived to the Spanish crown. When Hernando Pizarro went back to Spain in 1539, he was immediately imprisoned.

With Almagro's death, Pizarro had ostensibly consolidated power in Peru, but the reality was far more complex. At this point, a relatively large contingent of natives were siding with the Spaniards, such that in the pivotal battle of Ollantaytambo between Hernando Pizarro and Manco Inca, Pizarro had tens of thousands of indigenous allies under his command. Likewise, many Inca nobles in Cuzco had essentially capitulated to Spanish rule and tried to make the best of the new power arrangements. On the other hand, Manco was still attempting to reestablish his own power base. Eventually, he gave up on retaking Cuzco and led a large group of nobles and other natives loyal to him down the eastern slope of the Andes and into the jungle, where he established a kind of second Inca capital in exile. The city of Vilcabamba, as it was called, held out for several decades more, although Manco himself was murdered in 1544 by *almagrista* renegades to whom he had unwisely given refuge. In the meantime, Manco's brother Paullu Inca served as a puppet for the Spanish in Cuzco, ultimately accepting baptism under the name Cristóval and providing military support to both Almagro and the Pizarros on different occasions.

Even after Diego de Almagro's death, his supporters, led by his son Diego, continued to chafe under the rule of the Pizarros. Between them, Manco Inca's forces and the almagrista faction constituted two separate power bases that rendered Francisco Pizarro's position as governor and captain general of Peru highly vulnerable.

19th century painting of Diego de Almagro

Chapter 13: Ignoble Ends

Cortés would live more than 20 years after the conquest, and during those years his example would inspire many other Spaniards to seek their fortune in a similar way. The most successful of them was probably Francisco Pizarro, Cortés's second cousin, who would soon overcome an even larger empire to the south.

Cortés, on the other hand, would continue to reap benefits from his success, but his position would never again be quite as spectacular as it was in the wake of his defeat of the Aztecs. Although he had begun his campaign in a nearly treasonous manner, Charles V proved willing to forgive him his transgressions once he realized the wealth and scale of the newly subdued territory. He appointed Cortés governor of the entire Aztec empire, a position he was happy to assume since he no longer regarded his promises to allied native leaders as binding now once reinforcements were flooding in from Spain. The new name of the territory was to be New Spain. Cortés invited Franciscan friars to evangelize the population, and he began to establish the same *encomienda* system of labor practiced in the island territories. He continued the demolition of Aztec Tenochtitlán and began to build what would become Mexico City.

Once established firmly at the helm of the new colony, Cortés had no scruples about reneging on his promises to native allies, and he treated his own men nearly as poorly in some cases. They had come enticed by promises of wealth, but instead found themselves in debt to Cortés, who charged them for their use of weaponry he had supplied and for food, drink, and medical care. Meanwhile, merchants flooded in from Europe, selling goods at inflated prices. The disappointment suffered by many of those who fought with Cortés created a conflicted and tense environment and weakened the new governor's authority, even though it may have enriched him in the short term. Several of his former lieutenants set out on conquering expeditions on their own, hoping to recoup their losses and establish themselves independently as Cortés himself had done. One of them, Cristóbal de Olid, conspired with Cortés's old nemesis Diego Velázquez to take control of Honduras and rule it as his own territory. The attempt enraged Cortés, who had Olid captured and relieved of his command, but the conflict began a series of intrigues that pitted Cortés once more against Velázquez. Cortés clearly knew how to play the game, but Velázquez had far more influence in the Spanish court. The ultimate result was that Cortés was relieved of his governorship, exiled from the territory he had conquered, and sent back to Spain in 1528.

Cortés's remaining years were marked by repeated reversals of fortune. Sent back to Spain in a humiliating state, he was able to gain an audience with the crown. Successfully defending himself against various charges leveled by his enemies and rivals, he was honored by the king with a new title – Marquis of the Valley of Oaxaca – and a large *encomienda* in one of the wealthiest regions of New Spain. Despite these successes, he found himself with a reduced political stature when he returned to Mexico, not only because he was resented by many but because the crown, which was in the process of centralizing control over its American holdings, probably did not trust someone with his demonstrated ambitions to hold power responsibly. Already, the free-wheeling period of colonization in which he had taken part was giving way to the viceregal period, in which Spain would govern its overseas territories through a centralized and bureacratic administration in which individualists like Cortés would no longer thrive. In the late 1530s, perhaps attempting to relive his earlier triumphs, he set out on an expedition up the Pacific Coast, where he became among the first Europeans to reach Baja California.

Partly due to a conflict over his rights over the newly discovered territories and partly due to the lack of obvious wealth to be exploited there, Cortés eventually returned to central Mexico and then to Spain. His new exploratory mission had earned him a new crop of enemies in Mexico, and he probably hoped to obtain further support from the king. Instead, he received little recognition from Charles V, who was consumed with several wars in Europe and not terribly interested in his American holdings. In an attempt to win back the good grace of the sovereign, in 1541 he joined an expedition across the Mediterranean against the enemy Ottoman

Empire, but a subsequent attack on Algiers led to a disastrous rout of the Spanish forces, and Cortés barely escaped with his life. He lived much of the rest of his life racked with debts and embittered about his lack of recognition. He attempted to return to Mexico in late 1547, but fell ill in the port of Seville, where he died on December 2, 1547.

Pizarro had already met his own untimely end years earlier.

With Almagro dead and Manco in the distant jungle, Pizarro was at the height of his power and worldly success. By the end of the momentous decade of the 1530s, he was probably at least 65 and possibly near 70 years old, but he would not have the opportunity to enjoy his triumphs in peace in his later years. Instead, the man who rose to prominence by violence and treachery met a harsh but somewhat fitting end on June 26, 1541.

On that date, a group of about 20 conspirators under the leadership of the younger Diego de Almagro, who sought to avenge his father, broke into the governor's palace in Lima. The heavily armed attackers induced most of the palace guests to flee, while a handful stayed to fight. Even in his advanced age, Pizarro quickly tried to strap on his own breastplate and allegedly managed to kill a few of his attackers until the group started brutally stabbing him with swords. According to legend, Pizarro fell to the ground, formed a cross in his own blood and began praying. One of Spain's most notorious conquistadors was dead, and the conspirators proclaimed the young Almagro governor of Peru.

By the time of his death, Pizarro was not the most beloved leader to say the least. But he had just been murdered by the illegitimate offspring of Diego de Almagro and his indigenous mistress. Not surprisingly, the mestizo younger Almagro was not able to hold onto power for long. He would be dead within a year after Pizarro loyalists and reinforcements from Spain defeated him and the *almagristas* at the battle of Chupas in 1542. The younger Almagro was captured and executed.

Chapter 14: Legacies

Columbus

Among major historical figures, Christopher Columbus has held the rare distinction of being nearly all things to nearly all people. Since his death in Valladolid, Spain on May 20, 1506, his reputation has undergone an astonishing series of metamorphoses. At the time of his death, he had fallen into poverty and obscurity following the abject failures of his most recent expeditions across the ocean. He was only just beginning to acknowledge that he had not achieved the goal to which he had dedicated much of his life and fortune: the discovery of a westward maritime route to Asia. It would have surprised him, then, that his subsequent reputations, however varied, were all built on a very different accomplishment than the one he had sought for so long and ultimately fallen short of. Rather than the discoverer of new trade routes to China, India, and Japan, Columbus became, for later generations, the discoverer of a new continent, "America," which some proposed naming "Columbia" in his honor.

It would have been just as surprising to Columbus, perhaps, that he later became a national hero for Spain, given that his origins were in Genoa (now part of Italy) and his relations with the

Spanish crown, primarily commercial from the outset, had deteriorated by the time of his death. Perhaps more in line with his fervent religious inclinations would have been his later status as a hero of the Roman Catholic Church who had opened the path to evangelization for many thousands of new converts to the faith. But the unfolding of his many reputations would not end there. Columbus would also become a national hero of several of the republics of Spanish America, including one, Colombia, that would take his name as its own despite the fact that his historical relation to the place was highly tenuous: he had barely even skirted its coast during his several trajectories through the Caribbean Sea.

Perhaps most improbable of all, Columbus would also become a national hero, with a capital city and a national holiday in his honor, in the English-speaking republic to the north, whose territory he had never so much as glanced. There, he would be celebrated, with questionable accuracy, as a pioneer of science, entrepreneurialism, and individualism whose values anticipated those of the republic itself. In the meantime, he would also become a national and ethnic icon of the Italian nation and its various diasporic communities, despite the fact that such a thing as Italy did not exist until nearly four centuries after his death.

The story did not end, however, with Columbus's canonization as a patron saint of any number of nationalities, ethnicities, creeds, values, and ideals. In fact, when the 500th anniversary of his "discovery of America" arrived in 1992, something unexpected happened: people began to question whether it had in fact been a discovery at all. People had asked this question before, but it suddenly became the basis of a loud and emotional debate. After all, others had in fact discovered the land before him, and their descendants were living on it when he arrived. Shortly after his arrival, these inhabitants began to be massacred, enslaved, killed by imported diseases, and converted into second class citizens when they were allowed to remain on the land at all. Had not Columbus himself begun this process? Had he not begun the enslavement and killing on the first island where he established a settlement, which later, once the original inhabitants were all exterminated, became ground zero for the atrocities of African slavery? Was this a man whose deeds and legacy should be celebrated? Such questions led, in many quarters, to a devaluing of the previously sacrosanct reputation celebrated by the West, and thus was born the latest incarnation of Columbus: a villain and a racist, prototype of the colonialist warmonger, and ruthless capitalist exploiter of the Third World. This figure who once made people proud now, at best, makes them uncomfortable.

For a figure who has been subject to such remarkably diverse mythification, Columbus's actual life and career were in fact remarkably complex, mysterious, and equivocal. It is difficult, in light of the known facts of his life, to view him as an indisputable hero, as so many have done. The moral questions that have been raised about his celebrated activities and their consequences are surely both legitimate questions to ask of any historical figure and a valuable corrective to the lionization that had been prevalent for centuries. That they emerged was inevitable: for centuries, the lands opened up to European settlement by his explorations had been ruled mainly by white, Christian men like him, and it was only natural that they should see in him a forebear and a symbol of what they admired in themselves. But in the past half-century, people who were not white, not Christian, and/or not men have gained a great deal more influence on public debates, and it is not surprising that they might call into question the symbolism of a figure who played such a large role in allowing white, Christian men to rule over vast swaths of the earth, typically oppressing and marginalizing those were not like them.

On the other hand, it is somewhat unfair to convert Columbus into a scapegoat for the atrocities of the modern world. A more useful exercise is to attempt to situate Columbus within the larger processes that led to a world in which such things as colonialism and genocide became not only possible but in some periods routine. In doing so, it is possible to build a bridge between the world out of which Columbus emerged – a deeply religious late medieval world that is for the most part culturally and intellectually unfamiliar to contemporary readers – and the world that he helped create. For the world that he helped create is, simply put, today's world: a world of highly efficient communication and trade, but also one marked by perpetual conflict and rampant inequality, both driven in part by the legacies of conquest and colonialism. It makes no sense to selectively celebrate him for helping bring about the former or only blame him for the latter. Whatever today's world has of good and of bad, Columbus played an important role in making it that way.

Columbus's final legacy, then, was to have helped inaugurate one of the most momentous periods in world history, which would witness the rapid establishment of European power over two entire continents. Furthermore, his American exploration did open up new trade networks that ultimately (much as the explorer had hoped) gave Europe access to the riches of Asia, as well as those of the ruthlessly demolished empires of the Aztecs and the Incas. Further imperial enterprises, ultimately even more lucrative, would soon follow on the part of two of Spain's rivals, Britain and France, and the various regions of the world would become economically intertwined in way that few could have imagined in the 15th century. While debates over the exact nature of the man will continue to rage, by all estimates Columbus is a pivotal figure in the history of the ongoing phenomenon now known as globalization.

Cortés

A curious myth that sprung up in the immediate aftermath of his death claimed that Hernán Cortés, the conqueror of Mexico, had both been born and died on the same day and hour as Martin Luther, the founder of Protestantism. Moreover, this myth asserted, Cortés and Luther had led precisely parallel careers: while Luther had led much of Europe away from the Roman Catholic Church, Cortés had brought the people of a new continent into the Catholic fold; while Luther's reforms had deprived the Church of much of its property in Northern Europe, Cortés's conquest had filled the Church's coffers with untold quantities of gold.

As bizarre as it may appear at first, it is clear why such a myth made sense to the embattled Catholic Church of the mid-sixteenth century, which had recently, with the Protestant Reformation, felt its supremacy challenged from within for the first time in almost a thousand years. The parallel lives of Luther and Cortés proved that even though Satan was succeeding in undermining the Church through footsoldiers like Luther, God was counteracting the damage by way of appointed defenders of the faith such as Cortés. The latter's deeds were taken as proof of

God's providential plan for human history, which would lead ultimately to universal salvation.

The Cortés-Luther legend provides a vivid index of the deeply theological worldview of Christian Europe in the Age of Exploration, the period in which Cortés played such a pivotal role. The new – in this case, in the form of the new lands being explored and conquered in the New World, and the new faiths springing up in a formerly united Christendom – had to be incorporated into traditional frameworks so that it would confirm the teleological and apocalyptic Christian narrative that had long been promulgated by the Church and accepted in some form by most Europeans. In his book *The Old World and the New*, historian J.H. Elliott argues that it took some centuries for the genuine newness and difference of the Americas to be registered by European culture, so intent were most observers on finding ways of incorporating all new data into familiar narrative structures. Similarly, it can obviously be pointed out that it took some time for Cortés's career to be assessed historically, rather than theologically and morally.

On the other hand, there are some striking continuities between the initial accounts of Cortés's life that sprung up in his time and modern views of him: Protestants, for the most part, saw him as a villain and a scoundrel, proof of the tyrannical and brutal ways of the Catholic world at large, while many Catholics saw him as a hero of the faith. A similar split persists to this day: he is greatly despised for his ruthlessness, cunning, and dishonesty in many quarters, but for many still remains a heroic figure and paragon of remarkable individual accomplishments. Although Cortés was in fact born two years later than Luther and died more than a year after the famous reformer, the strange legend of their parallel lives contains the seed of an insight that most historians would accept today. Both Luther and Cortés were undoubtedly pivotal figures in the making of the modern world. Both struck out decisively beyond the horizons of medieval Catholicism and did so with a disregard of traditional authorities and hierarchies that set them apart from many of their peers. Both played a significant role in begetting a new culture: Luther, the individualistic, literate, and anti-hierarchical culture of Protestant Northern Europe, and Cortés, the conflicted but vital cultural and racial blend that would ultimately become modern Mexico and Latin America. Both also propelled the development of modern global capitalism: Luther, by fomenting a religious culture more propitious to the ambitions of merchants, traders, and moneylenders, and Cortés, by injecting the precious metals of the New World into the world economy. All in all, while they may have been regarded as opposite figures in their time, any account of the birth of the modern, globalized world that exists today could regard their roles as complementary.

While Cortés was certainly one of the most important figures in the history of the last millennium, he remains a difficult figure to admire as an individual, even if his daring and defiance are impressive. His personality was essentially that of a gambler, with all of the greed, egotism, and unscrupulousness that that suggests. The scion of a Spanish culture that claimed to venerate honor above all things, Cortés was remarkably short on that quality, and his success as a conqueror must be attributed in part to his willingness to break even the most basic rules of decency to achieve political and military victory. Throughout his career, he cheated, deceived, and manipulated those he wished to gain advantage over, and showed himself repeatedly willing to use deadly force against unarmed, friendly interlocutors. He even ripped off his own men, who had loyally and bravely followed him on a highly dangerous expedition. Indeed, as one historian has asserted, "Cortés's actions embodied the political concepts developed by Machiavelli" (Pastor 83).

It is impossible that Cortés could have read Machiavelli's seminal political treatise *The Prince*, but he seemed to have developed a parallel understanding of politics as a ruthless game of deception and cunning all on his own. In fact, his disregard for traditional morality and lack of scruples about the pursuit of worldly power makes him a progenitor of what has later come to be called *realpolitik*.

Pizarro

After his death, Pizarro continued to cast a long shadow over events in Peru and beyond for some time. Even as new settlers flooded in and royal administrators attempted to rein in the excesses of the colonists, members of Pizarro's family and of his original cohort of conquistadors continued to be protagonists in the violent conflicts that continued to consume the new colony for decades. His brother Gonzalo, in particular, was probably the foremost figure among the original generation of conquistadors for the entire decade of the 1540s. Before Francisco's death, Gonzalo was appointed governor of Quito, and from there he set out to the east, descending from the Andes into the Amazon basin along with the explorer Francisco de Orellana. The expedition became one of the most notoriously disastrous in the history of New World exploration, with its initial contingent of several hundred Spaniards and Indian porters suffering 50% casualties as a result of desertion, death by disease, hostile Indian attacks, and general harsh conditions. Nevertheless, Orellana ultimately became the first European to navigate the entire course of the Amazon River. His reports of warlike women on the shores of the great river were the inspiration of the name given to the river and the great basin it flows through.

Gonzalo, however, had left Orellana's expedition before it had reached the Amazon and returned to Quito. It was there that he learned of his brother's death at the hands of Almagro and his supporters, but he did not arrive in Lima in time to participate in the final routing of his family's great rivals. If he hoped that the defeat of the *almagristas* would put the Pizarro family back in charge of Peru, he was soon proven wrong. The crown, appalled by the infighting, chaos, and brutality that had consumed Peru since the conquest, had decided to impose a much greater centralized control and had shipped out a fleet of royal administrators and bureaucrats to do so.

This development was not unique to Peru. In general, the Spanish crown had grown tired of the way that the conquistadors had treated their conquered lands as personal fiefdoms and failed to show due deference to their monarchical overseers. Throughout Europe, moreover, this was a period of centralization in which the monarchy was consolidating its hold on power by reining in the traditional privileges of the aristocracy. The conquistadors, mostly of humble backgrounds, had set out to the New World in order to ascend to the coveted status of landed gentry. Now the entire existence of such a class was threatened by new regulation, and the dreams of men like Pizarro would become increasingly impossible to realize under the new system. The successful and powerful men of new imperial territories like Peru would from now on mainly consist of bureaucratic strivers, lawyers and clergymen who respected hierarchy and the chain of command in a way that the original settlers never had. In Pizarro's capital of Lima, this new form of authority would arrive in the person of Blasco Núñez Vela, the royally appointed first viceroy of Peru.

Blasco Núñez Vela

There were other over-arching developments that led to further conflict between the new viceroy and Gonzalo Pizarro, who saw himself as his brother's legitimate successor. One of Núñez Vela's orders was to enforce the recently passed New Laws, a surprisingly humanitarian piece of legislation that attempted to protect the indigenous peoples of the New World from

Spanish oppression. It is likely that the brutality of the Pizarros in Peru toward Atahualpa and his people played a role in winning over King Charles V to sign the new laws. They were also the result of the tireless campaigning of the Dominican friar Bartolomé de las Casas, who attacked the cruelty and rapacity of the Spanish conquistadors in unforgiving terms in a series of books, pamphlets, sermons, and public debates.

The New Laws aimed above all to reform the institution of the *encomienda*, which had played an important role in the conquest since Columbus's earliest settlements. Soldiers who participated in any conquest of new territory would be granted an *encomienda*, which was an "entrustment" of land with a certain number of natives whose labor they would be able to exploit by demanding tribute in exchange for instruction in Christianity. It was an essentially feudal arrangement, and it had led to the creation of *de facto* slavery throughout the colonies. The New Laws attempted to make indigenous peoples into free wage laborers and to significantly curtail the power of the *encomenderos*. It is debatable how much of the crown's motivation was humanitarian and how much the enforcement of natives' rights provided a convenient pretext for curtailing the disruptive power of the conquistadors and centralizing control over overseas territories, but the immediate results were more dramatic in their impact on the attitudes and loyalties of the Spanish colonists than on the lot of the natives.

The New Laws were only selectively enforced in the end, but their initial introduction to Peru was a scandal to all the original settlers who regarded themselves as having earned their power and positions through their military service. Making matters worse, Núñez arrived with orders to confiscate the property of anyone who had been directly involved in the feud between Pizarro and Almagro. Gonzalo Pizarro managed to unite most of the Spanish settlers in a rebellion against the New Laws and the viceroy, and he and in his supporters managed to kill Núñez in battle in 1546. At this point, Pizarro became unofficial ruler of Peru, and in a remarkable turn of events he and his followers decided to declare Peru an independent territory no longer under the rule of the King of Spain. Even more audaciously, Gonzalo named himself king of Peru, claiming that the Incas had legitimately abdicated power to his brother and he was the rightful successor. This was a remarkable turn of events given that Peru would not again seek independence for more than 250 years.

In 1547, a royal army arrived from Spain along with Pedro de la Gasca, who had been appointed as Núñez's replacement. De la Gasca shrewdly promised not to enforce the most onerous of the new laws, thus persuading a large contingent of colonists to withdraw their support from Gonzalo Pizarro's outlandish coup. Now the Spanish forces controlled Lima while Pizarro took refuge in Cuzco, where he had some loyalty among the colonists, veterans of his brother's campaigns, and some of the surviving Inca nobility who had intermarried with the conquistadors. But his base of support was small and dwindling now that the New Laws were less of a concern, and his forces were finally routed at the old Incan fortress of Sacsayhuamán, outside of Cuzco. He was beheaded by the victorious Spanish force. With his death in April 1548, the Pizarro family's hold on Peru was definitively broken, and the process of viceregal centralization had succeeded.

Pedro de la Gasca

    The defiant faction of Incas at the Amazonian stronghold of Vilcabamba held out considerably longer in their bid for independence from Spanish control. After Manco Inca's murder, Manco's son Sayri Tupac succeeded him and ruled for over ten years until finally returning to Cuzco and submitting to the new order. His brother Titu Cusi took over and remained in power until 1571, trying to maintain friendly relations with the Spaniards and even accepting Christian baptism. After his death, he was succeeded by his younger brother Tupac Amaru.

    Around the same time, two Spanish emissaries were killed in the jungle near Vilcabamba, and this gave the viceroy, Francisco de Toledo, the pretext he needed to declare war against the troublesome enclave of holdouts. He sent an expeditionary force into the difficult jungle terrain and, despite difficulties, they drove Tupac Amaru out of Vilcabamba and captured him and much of his entourage, along with the remains of the two previous emperors and several sacred objects.

The latter were taken to Cuzco and burned as idols and as a warning to any sympathizers among the surviving natives. Tupac Amaru, like Gonzalo Pizarro, was beheaded. As with the executions of Atahualpa and Diego de Almagro, the punishment was controversial: priests, administrators, and finally the Spanish king himself all objected to Toledo's act. But it was done, and now the last vestige of the Inca power structure was gone. It is a surprising and little-known fact that, despite the apparently decisive blow dealt to the Incas by Pizarro's murder of Atahualpa, the Inca state had remained in existence in modified form for nearly 40 years afterwards.

The Dominican friar Bartolomé de Las Casas (c. 1484-1566), who had first-hand experience witnessing the actions of the Spanish conquistadors, damned Pizarro for his cruelty in destroying the Inca Empire. In his *Short Account of the Destruction of the Indies,* written in 1542, Las Casas described Pizzaro's violent rampage in search of gold, writing that he "criminally murdered and plundered his way through the region, razing towns and cities to the ground and slaughtering and otherwise tormenting in the most barbaric fashion imaginable the people who lived there." As evidence of the crimes, Las Casas quoted an affidavit sworn by the Franciscan Brother Marcos de Niza, who was present during Pizarro's conquest. Among many atrocities Brother Marcos wrote, "I testify that I saw with my own eyes Spaniards cutting off the hands, noses and ears of local people, both men and women, simply for the fun of it."

Peru would go onto become the wealthiest of Spain's colonies, with the inhabitants of Lima living in legendary opulence even as the wealth was built on the back of impoverished Indian labor that was usually difficult to distinguish from slavery. The New Laws remained largely unenforced, and the harsh treatment of the Indians employed in agriculture and mining led to a number of rebellions. The first that truly shook Spain's hold on power was led by a man who assumed the title of Tupac Amaru II. Even after Peru gained independence from Spain in 1824, the highly unequal political and economic system first created by Pizarro remained largely intact. The capital of Lima remained the center of power, with much of its wealthy and middle class of Spanish or other European stock, while the vast indigenous majority remained in the Andean mountains, living in practically feudal conditions.

Only in recent years, especially with mass migration of indigenous people from the countryside into the large cities, has the traditional power structure begun to shift somewhat, a development perhaps most clearly signaled by the election of Peru's first indigenous president, Alejandro Toledo, in 2001. Francisco Pizarro's most significant ongoing legacy, much like his most significant immediate legacy, is a conflict over power and resources. This conflict will continue to consume Peru and the other countries built on former Inca territories (Ecuador, Bolivia) until the inequalities first put in place by the conquistadors and perpetuated by the Spanish colonial governments have been resolved.

Compared to other notables of what has come to be known as the Age of Exploration, Francisco Pizarro enjoys a less than assured reputation. His relative neglect is somewhat surprising in a number of ways, but it can probably be explained on the basis of several factors. If judged purely on the basis of what many of his contemporaries sought in the period of his activity – adventure, military triumph, land, and wealth – Pizarro probably outstrips all of them. After all, Christopher Columbus, who has a country named after him and whose deeds are celebrated on holidays in dozens of countries, never even set out to discover previously unknown lands: he wished to reach Asia and tap into the lucrative Indian Ocean spice trade. He not only failed in this endeavor but ended up being expelled from the one colony he did found (Hispaniola), and he never reached a land abundant with the kind of resources he expected. Hernán Cortés subdued the powerful and wealthy Aztec empire, but his reign as governor of the new Spanish colony he founded was short and controversial. While he remained relatively wealthy, he died embittered, like Columbus, from a sense of not being appreciated by the powers whose interests he had served. Ferdinand Magellan succeeded where Columbus had failed: he reached Asia by a westward route, giving the Portuguese crown privileged access to the spice and silk trades. But even though he is (ironically) remembered as the man who circumnavigated the globe, Magellan died in the Philippines during his famous journey, thus unable to enjoy any glory.

Pizarro's last years and death were certainly as fraught as those of the contemporaries just named – he was ultimately murdered by mutinous Spaniards drawn from among his own former comrades in arms – but his military achievements were if anything more remarkable than those of Cortés, at least in so far as the empire he overthrew was larger, wealthier, and better prepared in military terms. By establishing a foothold on the central ridge of the Andes, he also opened up immense new territories for Spanish imperial expansion, which would soon encompass most of the South American continent. The Spanish presence in Mexico, in contrast, did not lead to a massive expansion into North America on the same scale. Lima, the city Pizarro founded on the coast of Peru in 1535, would go on to become one of the wealthiest cities in the world for a time, on the strength of the unimaginably vast silver and gold deposits of the Andes. Even more than the precious metals of Mexico, the wealth of Peru exploited by Pizarro and his successors would have a dramatic and lasting impact on the global economy, and arguably it was a primary impetus for the growth of modern European capitalism

Although they were distantly related through Cortés's mother, Doña Catalina Pizarro, Francisco Pizarro was of a lower social rank than Cortés, who came from modest means but possessed a legitimately aristocratic lineage on both sides. An illegitimate child, he had been a humble swineherd before setting off to the Indies in the hope of bettering his lot. Perhaps even more significantly, Pizarro possessed little education and was either illiterate or barely literate. Cortés, in contrast, had attended the prestigious University of Salamanca and, as a trained notary and magistrate, was a sophisticated rhetorician whose finely phrased letters to the monarchy won him support and admiration, not least from the historian Francisco López de Gómara, who wrote a glowing biography of the conqueror of Mexico. To put it differently, while Cortés and Pizarro did much the same thing, the former did so with greater literary flourish, and the result has been a lasting aura of heroism and boldness that has eluded the latter. Finally, Pizarro died even more ignominiously than Cortés or Columbus, having overseen the descent of his new Spanish colony into a vicious civil war and been murdered by the son of his former business partner.

In truth, and especially from a 21st century vantage point, it is hard to find much to admire in either Cortés or Pizarro. Both were venal, conniving, and brutal; both achieved much of what they accomplished through a combination of treachery and callous disregard for human life; both have on their hands the practical destruction of an entire civilization. Not surprisingly, in modern Peru, Pizarro is not even remotely a national hero. For perhaps the majority of the Peruvian population, descended partly or fully from the indigenous groups he and the other Spanish conquerors subjugated and essentially enslaved, he is regarded as an invader and an illegitimate ruler whose actions set the country on a catastrophic path. And indeed, the inequalities of the colonial order he established, in which the indigenous people became largely subservient to the Spanish conquerors, still remain a fact of life: most of Peru's wealthiest citizens are of European descent, while its poorest people are almost universally of indigenous background. In the capital city of Lima, popular repudiation recently forced the government to move an equestrian statue of Pizarro away from the central plaza and to a less central location. Like the other conquistadors, Pizarro's legacy has declined even moreso since 1992, the quincentennial of Columbus's landfall in the Indies. In addition to helping Columbus retain the spotlight, that year's commemoration was a watershed moment for alternative versions of history, in which the experiences of the native peoples who experienced the consequences of Spanish aggression and greed took precedence over traditional narratives of conquering heroes. It can be safely assumed that Native American perception of Pizarro will not improve anytime soon.

Extracts from Columbus's Journal of His First Voyage

This document is from the journal of Columbus in his voyage of 1492. The meaning of this voyage is highly contested. On the one hand, it is witness to the tremendous vitality and verve of late medieval and early modern Europe - which was on the verge of acquiring a world hegemony. On the other hand, the direct result of this and later voyages was the virtual extermination, by ill-treatment and disease, of the vast majority of the Native inhabitants, and the enormous growth of the transatlantic slave trade. It might not be fair to lay the blame at Columbus' feet, but since all sides treat him as a symbol, such questions cannot be avoided.

IN THE NAME OF OUR LORD JESUS CHRIST

Whereas, Most Christian, High, Excellent, and Powerful Princes, King and Queen of Spain and of the Islands of the Sea, our Sovereigns, this present year 1492, after your Highnesses had terminated the war with the Moors reigning in Europe, the same having been brought to an end in the great city of Granada, where on the second day of January, this present year, I saw the royal banners of your Highnesses planted by force of arms upon the towers of the Alhambra, which is the fortress of that city, and saw the Moorish king come out at the gate of the city and kiss the hands of your Highnesses, and of the Prince my Sovereign; and in the present month, in consequence of the information which I had given your Highnesses respecting the countries of India and of a Prince, called Great Can, which in our language signifies King of Kings, how, at many times he, and his predecessors had sent to Rome soliciting instructors who might teach him our holy faith, and the holy Father had never granted his request, whereby great numbers of people were lost, believing in idolatry and doctrines of perdition. Your Highnesses, as Catholic Christians, and princes who love and promote the holy Christian faith, and are enemies of the doctrine of Mahomet, and of all idolatry and heresy, determined to send me, Christopher Columbus, to the above-mentioned countries of India, to see the said princes, people, and territories, and to learn their disposition and the proper method of converting them to our holy faith; and furthermore directed that I should not proceed by land to the East, as is customary, but by a Westerly route, in which direction we have hitherto no certain evidence that any one has gone. So after having expelled the Jews from your dominions, your Highnesses, in the same month of January, ordered me to proceed with a sufficient armament to the said regions of India, and for that purpose granted me great favors, and ennobled me that thenceforth I might call myself Don, and be High Admiral of the Sea, and perpetual Viceroy and Governor in all the islands and continents which I might discover and acquire, or which may hereafter he discovered and acquired in the ocean; and that this dignity should be inherited by my eldest son, and thus descend from degree to degree forever. Hereupon I left the city of Granada, on Saturday, the twelfth day of May, 1492, and proceeded to Palos, a seaport, where I armed three vessels, very fit for such an enterprise, and having provided myself with abundance of stores and seamen, I set sail from the port, on Friday, the third of August, half an hour before sunrise, and steered for the Canary Islands of your Highnesses which are in the said ocean, thence to take my departure and proceed till I arrived at the Indies, and perform the embassy of your Highnesses to the Princes there, and discharge the orders given me. For this purpose I determined to keep an account of the voyage, and to write down punctually every thing we performed or saw from day to day, as will hereafter appear. Moreover, Sovereign Princes, besides describing every night the occurrences of the day, and every day those of the preceding night, I intend to draw up a nautical chart, which shall contain the several parts of the ocean and land in their proper situations; and also to compose a book to represent the whole by picture with latitudes and longitudes, on all which accounts it behooves me to abstain from my sleep, and make many trials in navigation, which things will demand much labor.

Friday, 3 August 1492. Set sail from the bar of Saltes at 8 o'clock, and proceeded with a strong breeze till sunset, sixty miles or fifteen leagues south, afterwards southwest and south by west, which is the direction of the Canaries.

* * * * *

Monday, 6 August. The rudder of the caravel Pinta became loose, being broken or unshipped. It was believed that this happened by the contrivance of Gomez Rascon and Christopher Quintero, who were on board the caravel, because they disliked the voyage. The Admiral says he had found them in an unfavorable disposition before setting out. He was in much anxiety at not being able to afford any assistance in this case, but says that it somewhat quieted his apprehensions to know that Martin Alonzo Pinzon, Captain of the Pinta, was a man of courage and capacity. Made a progress, day and night, of twenty-nine leagues.

* * * * *

Thursday, 9 August. The Admiral did not succeed in reaching the island of Gomera till Sunday night. Martin Alonzo remained at Grand Canary by command of the Admiral, he being unable to keep the other vessels company. The Admiral afterwards returned to Grand Canary, and there with much labor repaired the Pinta, being assisted by Martin Alonzo and the others; finally they sailed to Gomera. They saw a great eruption of names from the Peak of Teneriffe, a lofty mountain. The Pinta, which before had carried latine sails, they altered and made her square-rigged. Returned to Gomera, Sunday, 2 September, with the Pinta repaired.

The Admiral says that he was assured by many respectable Spaniards, inhabitants of the island of Ferro, who were at Gomera with Dona Inez Peraza, mother of Guillen Peraza, afterwards first Count of Gomera, that every year they saw land to the west of the Canaries; and others of Gomera affirmed the same with the like assurances. The Admiral here says that he remembers, while he was in Portugal, in 1484, there came a person to the King from the island of Madeira, soliciting for a vessel to go in quest of land, which he affirmed he saw every year, and always of the same appearance. He also says that he remembers the same was said by the inhabitants of the Azores and described as in a similar direction, and of the same shape and size. Having taken in food, water, meat and other provisions, which had been provided by the men which he left ashore on departing for Grand Canary to repair the Pinta, the Admiral took his final departure from Gomera with the three vessels on Thursday, 6 September.

* * * * *

Sunday, 9 September. Sailed this day nineteen leagues, and determined to count less than the true number, that the crew might not be dismayed if the voyage should prove long. In the night sailed one hundred and twenty miles, at the rate of ten miles an hour, which make thirty leagues. The sailors steered badly, causing the vessels to fall to leeward toward the northeast, for which the Admiral reprimanded them repeatedly.

Monday, 10 September. This day and night sailed sixty leagues, at the rate of ten miles an hour, which are two leagues and a half. Reckoned only forty-eight leagues, that the men might not be terrified if they should be long upon the voyage.

Tuesday, 11 September. Steered their course west and sailed above twenty leagues; saw a large fragment of the mast of a vessel, apparently of a hundred and twenty tons, but could not pick it up. In the night sailed about twenty leagues, and reckoned only sixteen, for the cause above stated.

* * * * *

Friday, 14 September. Steered this day and night west twenty leagues; reckoned somewhat less. The crew of the Nina stated that they had seen a grajao, and a tropic bird, or water-wagtail, which birds never go farther than twenty-five leagues from the land.

* * * * *

Sunday, 16 September. Sailed day and night, west thirty-nine leagues, and reckoned only thirty-six. Some clouds arose and it drizzled. The Admiral here says that from this time they experienced very pleasant weather, and that the mornings were most delightful, wanting nothing but the melody of the nightingales. He compares the weather to that of Andalusia in April. Here they began to meet with large patches of weeds very green, and which appeared to have been recently washed away from the land; on which account they all judged themselves to be near some island, though not a continent, according to the opinion of the Admiral, who says, "the continent we shall find further ahead."

Monday, 17 September. Steered west and sailed, day and night, above fifty leagues; wrote down only forty-seven; the current favored them. They saw a great deal of weed which proved to be rockweed, it came from the west and they met with it very frequently. They were of opinion that land was near. The pilots took the sun's amplitude, and found that the needles varied to the northwest a whole point of the compass; the seamen were terrified, and dismayed without saying why. The Admiral discovered the cause, and ordered them to take the amplitude again the next morning, when they found that the needles were true; the cause was that the star moved from its place, while the needles remained stationary. At dawn they saw many more weeds, apparently river weeds, and among them a live crab, which the Admiral kept, and says that these are sure signs of land, being never found eighty leagues out at sea. They found the sea-water less salt since they left the Canaries, and the air milder. They were all very cheerful, and strove which vessel should outsail the others, and be the first to discover land; they saw many tunnies, and the crew of the Nina killed one. The Admiral here says that these signs were from the west, "where I hope that high God in whose hand is all victory will speedily direct us to land." This morning he says he saw a white bird called a water- wagtail, or tropic bird, which does not sleep at sea.

* * * * *

19 September. Continued on, and sailed, day and night, twenty- five leagues, experiencing a calm. Wrote down twenty-two. This day at ten o'clock a pelican came on board, and in the evening another; these birds are not accustomed to go twenty leagues from land. It drizzled without wind, which is a sure sign of land. The Admiral was unwilling to remain here, beating about in search of land, but he held it for certain that there were islands to the north and south, which in fact was the case and he was sailing in the midst of them. His wish was to proceed on to

the Indies, having such fair weather, for if it please God, as the Admiral says, we shall examine these parts upon our return. Here the pilots found their places upon the chart: the reckoning of the Nina made her four hundred and forty leagues distant from the Canaries, that of the Pinta four hundred and twenty, that of the Admiral four hundred.

Thursday, 20 September. Steered west by north, varying with alternate changes of the wind and calms; made seven or eight leagues' progress. Two pelicans came on board, and afterwards another,--a sign of the neighborhood of land. Saw large quantities of weeds today, though none was observed yesterday. Caught a bird similar to a grajao; it was a river and not a marine bird, with feet like those of a gull. Towards night two or three land birds came to the ship, singing; they disappeared before sunrise. Afterwards saw a pelican coming from west- northwest and flying to the southwest; an evidence of land to the westward, as these birds sleep on shore, and go to sea in the morning in search of food, never proceeding twenty leagues from the land.

Friday, 21 September. Most of the day calm, afterwards a little wind. Steered their course day and night, sailing less than thirteen leagues. In the morning found such abundance of weeds that the ocean seemed to be covered with them; they came from the west. Saw a pelican; the sea smooth as a river, and the finest air in the world. Saw a whale, an indication of land, as they always keep near the coast.

Saturday, 22 September. Steered about west-northwest varying their course, and making thirty leagues' progress. Saw few weeds. Some pardelas were seen, and another bird. The Admiral here says "this headwind was very necessary to me, for my crew had grown much alarmed, dreading that they never should meet in these seas with a fair wind to return to Spain." Part of the day saw no weeds, afterwards great plenty of it.

Sunday, 23 September. Sailed northwest and northwest by north and at times west nearly twenty-two leagues. Saw a turtle dove, a pelican, a river bird, and other white fowl;--weeds in abundance with crabs among them. The sea being smooth and tranquil, the sailors murmured, saying that they had got into smooth water, where it would never blow to carry them back to Spain; but afterwards the sea rose without wind, which astonished them. The Admiral says on this occasion "the rising of the sea was very favorable to me, as it happened formerly to Moses when he led the Jews from Egypt."

* * * * *

Tuesday, 25 September. Very calm this day; afterwards the wind rose. Continued their course west till night. The Admiral held a conversation with Martin Alonzo Pinzon, captain of the Pinta, respecting a chart which the Admiral had sent him three days before, in which it appears he had marked down certain islands in that sea; Martin Alonzo was of opinion that they were in their neighborhood, and the Admiral replied that he thought the same, but as they had not met with them, it must have been owing to the currents which had carried them to the northeast and that they had not made such progress as the pilots stated. The Admiral directed him to return the chart, when he traced their course upon it in presence of the pilot and sailors.

At sunset Martin Alonzo called out with great joy from his vessel that he saw land, and demanded of the Admiral a reward for his intelligence. The Admiral says, when he heard him declare this, he fell on his knees and returned thanks to God, and Martin Alonzo with his crew repeated Gloria in excelsis Deo, as did the crew of the Admiral. Those on board the Nina ascended the rigging, and all declared they saw land. The Admiral also thought it was land, and about twenty-five leagues distant. They remained all night repeating these affirmations, and the Admiral ordered their course to be shifted from west to southwest where the land appeared to lie. They sailed that day four leagues and a half west and in the night seventeen leagues southwest, in all twenty-one and a half: told the crew thirteen leagues, making it a point to keep them from knowing how far they had sailed; in this manner two reckonings were kept, the shorter one falsified, and the other being the true account. The sea was very smooth and many of the sailors went in it to bathe, saw many dories and other fish.

Wednesday, 26 September. Continued their course west till the afternoon, then southwest and discovered that what they had taken for land was nothing but clouds. Sailed, day and night, thirty- one leagues; reckoned to the crew twenty-four. The sea was like a river, the air soft and mild.

* * * * *

Sunday, 30 September. Continued their course west and sailed day and night in calms, fourteen leagues; reckoned eleven.--Four tropic birds came to the ship, which is a very clear sign of land, for so many birds of one sort together show that they are not straying about, having lost themselves. Twice, saw two pelicans; many weeds. The constellation called Las Gallardias, which at evening appeared in a westerly direction, was seen in the northeast the next morning, making no more progress in a night of nine hours, this was the case every night, as says the Admiral. At night the needles varied a point towards the northwest, in the morning they were true, by which it appears that the polar star moves, like the others, and the needles are always right.

Monday, 1 October. Continued their course west and sailed twenty-five leagues; reckoned to the crew twenty. Experienced a heavy shower. The pilot of the Admiral began to fear this morning that they were five hundred and seventy-eight leagues west of the island of Ferro. The short reckoning which the Admiral showed his crew gave five hundred and eighty-four, but the true one which he kept to himself was seven hundred and seven leagues.

* * * * *

Saturday, 6 October. Continued their course west and sailed forty leagues day and night; reckoned to the crew thirty-three. This night Martin Alonzo gave it as his opinion that they had better steer from west to southwest. The Admiral thought from this that Martin Alonzo did not wish to proceed onward to Cipango; but he considered it best to keep on his course, as he should probably reach the land sooner in that direction, preferring to visit the continent first, and then the islands.

Sunday, 7 October. Continued their course west and sailed twelve miles an hour, for two hours, then eight miles an hour. Sailed till an hour after sunrise, twenty-three leagues; reckoned to the crew eighteen. At sunrise the caravel Nina, who kept ahead on account of her swiftness in sailing, while all the vessels were striving to outsail one another, and gain the reward promised by the King and Queen by first discovering land--hoisted a flag at her mast head, and fired a lombarda, as a signal that she had discovered land, for the Admiral had given orders to that effect. He had also ordered that the ships should keep in close company at sunrise and sunset, as the air was more favorable at those times for seeing at a distance. Towards evening seeing nothing of the land which the Nina had made signals for, and observing large flocks of birds coming from the North and making for the southwest, whereby it was rendered probable that they were either going to land to pass the night, or abandoning the countries of the north, on account of the approaching winter, he determined to alter his course, knowing also that the Portuguese had discovered most of the islands they possessed by attending to the flight of birds. The Admiral accordingly shifted his course from west to west-southwest, with a resolution to continue two days ill that direction. This was done about an hour after sunset. Sailed in the night nearly five leagues, and twenty-three in the day. In all twenty-eight.

8 October. Steered west-southwest and sailed day and night eleven or twelve leagues; at times during the night, fifteen miles an hour, if the account can be depended upon. Found the sea like the river at Seville, "thanks to God," says the Admiral. The air soft as that of Seville in April, and so fragrant that it was delicious to breathe it. The weeds appeared very fresh. Many land birds, one of which they took, flying towards the southwest; also grajaos, ducks, and a pelican were seen.

Tuesday, 9 October. Sailed southwest five leagues, when the wind changed, and they stood west by north four leagues. Sailed in the whole day and night, twenty leagues and a half; reckoned to the crew seventeen. All night heard birds passing.

Wednesday, 10 October. Steered west-southwest and sailed at times ten miles an hour, at others twelve, and at others, seven; day and night made fifty-nine leagues' progress; reckoned to the crew but forty-four. Here the men lost all patience, and complained of the length of the voyage, but the Admiral encouraged them in the best manner he could, representing the profits they were about to acquire, and adding that it was to no purpose to complain, having come so far, they had nothing to do but continue on to the Indies, till with the help of our Lord, they should arrive there.

Thursday, 11 October. Steered west-southwest; and encountered a heavier sea than they had met with before in the whole voyage. Saw pardelas and a green rush near the vessel. The crew of the Pinta saw a cane and a log; they also picked up a stick which appeared to have been carved with an iron tool, a piece of cane, a plant which grows on land, and a board. The crew of the Nina saw other signs of land, and a stalk loaded with rose berries. These signs encouraged them, and they all grew cheerful. Sailed this day till sunset, twenty-seven leagues.

After sunset steered their original course west and sailed twelve miles an hour till two hours after midnight, going ninety miles, which are twenty-two leagues and a half; and as the Pinta was the swiftest sailer, and kept ahead of the Admiral, she discovered land and made the signals which had been ordered. The land was first seen by a sailor called Rodrigo de Triana, although the Admiral at ten o'clock that evening standing on the quarter-deck saw a light, but so small a body that he could not affirm it to be land; calling to Pero Gutierrez, groom of the King's wardrobe, he told him he saw a light, and bid him look that way, which he did and saw it; he did the same to Rodrigo Sanchez of Segovia, whom the King and Queen had sent with the squadron as comptroller, but he was unable to see it from his situation. The Admiral again perceived it once or twice, appearing like the light of a wax candle moving up and down, which some thought an indication of land. But the Admiral held it for certain that land was near; for which reason, after they had said the Salve which the seamen are accustomed to repeat and chant after their fashion, the Admiral directed them to keep a strict watch upon the forecastle and look out diligently for land, and to him who should first discover it he promised a silken jacket, besides the reward which the King and Queen had offered, which was an annuity of ten thousand maravedis. At two o'clock in the morning the land was discovered, at two leagues' distance; they took in sail and remained under the square-sail lying to till day, which was Friday, when they found themselves near a small island, one of the Lucayos, called in the Indian language Guanahani. Presently they descried people, naked, and the Admiral landed in the boat, which was armed, along with Martin Alonzo Pinzon, and Vincent Yanez his brother, captain of the Nina. The Admiral bore the royal standard, and the two captains each a banner of the Green Cross, which all the ships had carried; this contained the initials of the names of the King and Queen each side of the cross, and a crown over each letter Arrived on shore, they saw trees very green many streams of water, and diverse sorts of fruits. The Admiral called upon the two Captains, and the rest of the crew who landed, as also to Rodrigo de Escovedo notary of the fleet, and Rodrigo Sanchez, of Segovia, to bear witness that he before all others took possession (as in fact he did) of that island for the King and Queen his sovereigns, making the requisite declarations, which are more at large set down here in writing. Numbers of the people of the island straightway collected together. Here follow the precise words of the Admiral: "As I saw that they were very friendly to us, and perceived that they could be much more easily converted to our holy faith by gentle means than by force, I presented them with some red caps, and strings of beads to wear upon the neck, and many other trifles of small value, wherewith they were much delighted, and became wonderfully attached to us. Afterwards they came swimming to the boats, bringing parrots, balls of cotton thread, javelins, and many other things which they exchanged for articles we gave them, such as glass beads, and hawk's bells; which trade was carried on with the utmost good will. But they seemed on the whole to me, to be a very poor people. They all go completely naked, even the women, though I saw but one girl. All whom I saw were young, not above thirty years of age, well made, with fine shapes and faces; their hair short, and coarse like that of a horse's tail, combed toward the forehead, except a small portion which they suffer to hang down behind, and never cut. Some paint themselves with black, which makes them appear like those of the Canaries, neither black nor white; others with white, others with red, and others with such colors as they can find. Some paint the face, and some the whole body; others only the eyes, and others the nose. Weapons they have none, nor are acquainted with them, for I showed them swords which they grasped by the blades, and cut themselves through ignorance. They have no iron, their javelins being without it, and nothing more than sticks, though some have fish-bones or other things at the ends. They are all of a good size and stature, and handsomely formed. I saw some with scars of wounds upon their bodies, and demanded by signs the of them; they answered me in the same way, that there came people from the other islands in the neighborhood who endeavored to make prisoners of them, and they defended themselves. I thought then, and still believe, that these were from the continent. It appears to me, that the people are ingenious, and would be good servants and I am of opinion that they would very readily become Christians, as they appear to have no religion. They very quickly learn such words as are spoken to them. If it please our Lord, I intend at my return to carry home six of them to your Highnesses, that they may learn our language. I saw no beasts in the island, nor any sort of animals except parrots." These are the words of the Admiral.

Saturday, 13 October. "At daybreak great multitudes of men came to the shore, all young and of fine shapes, very handsome; their hair not curled but straight and coarse like horse-hair, and all with foreheads and heads much broader than any people I had hitherto seen; their eyes were large and very beautiful; they were not black, but the color of the inhabitants of the Canaries, which is a very natural circumstance, they being in the same latitude with the island of Ferro in the Canaries. They were straight-limbed without exception, and not with prominent bellies but handsomely shaped. They came to the ship in canoes, made of a single trunk of a tree, wrought in a wonderful manner considering the country; some of them large enough to contain forty or forty-five men, others of different sizes down to those fitted to hold but a single person. They rowed with an oar like a baker's peel, and wonderfully swift. If they happen to upset, they all jump into the sea, and swim till they have righted their canoe and emptied it with the calabashes they carry with them. They came loaded with balls of cotton, parrots, javelins, and other things too numerous to mention; these they exchanged for whatever we chose to give them. I was very attentive to them, and strove to learn if they had any gold. Seeing some of them with little bits of this metal hanging at their noses, I gathered from them by signs that by going southward or steering round the island in that direction, there would be found a king who possessed large vessels of gold, and in great quantities. I endeavored to procure them to lead the way thither, but found they were unacquainted with the route. I determined to stay here till the evening of the next day, and then sail for the southwest; for according to what I could learn from them, there was land at the south as well as at the southwest and northwest and those from the northwest came many times and fought with them and proceeded on to the southwest in search of gold and precious stones. This is a large and level island, with trees extremely flourishing, and streams of water; there is a large lake in the middle of the island, but no mountains: the whole is completely covered with verdure and delightful to behold. The natives are an inoffensive people, and so desirous to possess any thing they saw with us, that they kept swimming off to the ships with whatever they could find, and readily bartered for any article we saw fit to give them in return, even such as broken platters and fragments of glass. I saw in this manner sixteen balls of cotton thread which weighed above twenty-five pounds, given for three Portuguese ceutis. This traffic I forbade, and suffered no one to take their cotton from them, unless I should order it to be procured for your Highnesses, if proper quantities could be met with. It grows in this island, but from my short stay here I could not satisfy myself fully concerning it; the gold, also, which they wear in their noses, is found here, but not to lose time, I am determined to proceed onward and ascertain whether I can reach Cipango. At night they all went on shore with their canoes.

Sunday, 14 October. In the morning, I ordered the boats to be got ready, and coasted along the island toward the north- northeast to examine that part of it, we having landed first at the eastern part. Presently we discovered two or three villages, and the people all came down to the shore, calling out to us, and giving thanks to God. Some brought us water, and others victuals: others seeing that I was not disposed to land, plunged into the sea and swam out to us, and we perceived that they interrogated us if we had come from heaven. An old man came on board my boat; the others, both men and women cried with loud voices--"Come and see the men who have come from heavens. Bring them victuals and drink." There came many of both sexes, every one bringing something, giving thanks to God, prostrating themselves on the earth, and lifting up their hands to heaven. They called out to us loudly to come to land, but I was apprehensive on account of a reef of rocks, which surrounds the whole island, although within there is depth of water and room sufficient for all the ships of Christendom, with a very narrow entrance. There are some shoals withinside, but the water is as smooth as a pond. It was to view these parts that I set out in the morning, for I wished to give a complete relation to your Highnesses, as also to find where a fort might be built. I discovered a tongue of land which appeared like an island though it was not, but might be cut through and made so in two days; it contained six houses. I do not, however, see the necessity of fortifying the place, as the people here are simple in war-like matters, as your Highnesses will see by those seven which I have ordered to be taken and carried to Spain in order to learn our language and return, unless your Highnesses should choose to have them all transported to Castile, or held captive in the island. I could conquer the whole of them with fifty men, and govern them as I pleased. Near the islet I have mentioned were groves of trees, the most beautiful I have ever seen, with their foliage as verdant as we see in Castile in April and May. There were also many streams. After having taken a survey of these parts, I returned to the ship, and setting sail, discovered such a number of islands that I knew not which first to visit; the natives whom I had taken on board informed me by signs that there were so many of them that they could not be numbered; they repeated the names of more than a hundred. I determined to steer for the largest, which is about five leagues from San Salvador; the others were some at a greater, and some at a less distance from that island. They are all very level, without mountains, exceedingly fertile and populous, the inhabitants living at war with one another, although a simple race, and with delicate bodies.

15 October. Stood off and on during the night, determining not to come to anchor till morning, fearing to meet with shoals; continued our course in the morning; and as the island was found to be six or seven leagues distant, and the tide was against us, it was noon when we arrived there. I found that part of it towards San Salvador extending from north to south five leagues, and the other side which we coasted along, ran from east to west more than ten leagues. From this island espying a still larger one to the west, I set sail in that direction and kept on till night without reaching the western extremity of the island, where I gave it the name of Santa Maria de la Concepcion. About sunset we anchored near the cape which terminates the island towards the west to enquire for gold, for the natives we had taken from San Salvador told me that the people here wore golden bracelets upon their arms and legs. I believed pretty confidently that they had invented this story in order to find means to escape from us, still I determined to pass none of these islands without taking possession, because being once taken, it would answer for all times. We anchored and remained till Tuesday, when at daybreak I went ashore with the boats armed. The people we found naked like those of San Salvador, and of the same disposition. They suffered us to traverse the island, and gave us what we asked of them. As the wind blew southeast upon the shore where the vessels lay, I determined not to remain, and set out for the ship. A large canoe being near the caravel Nina, one of the San Salvador natives leaped overboard and swam to her; (another had made his escape the night before,) the canoe being reached by the fugitive, the natives rowed for the land too swiftly to be overtaken; having landed, some of my men went ashore in pursuit of them, when they abandoned the canoe and fled with precipitation; the canoe which they had left was brought on board the Nina, where from another quarter had arrived a small canoe with a single man, who came to barter some cotton; some of the sailors finding him unwilling to go on board the vessel, jumped into the sea and took him. I was upon the quarter deck of my ship, and seeing the whole, sent for him, and gave him a red cap, put some glass beads upon his arms, and two hawk's bells upon his ears. I then ordered his canoe to be returned to him, and despatched him back to land.

I now set sail for the other large island to the west and gave orders for the canoe which the Nina had in tow to be set adrift. I had refused to receive the cotton from the native whom I sent on shore, although he pressed it upon me. I looked out after him and saw upon his landing that the others all ran to meet him with much wonder. It appeared to them that we were honest people, and that the man who had escaped from us had done us some injury, for which we kept him in custody. It was in order to favor this notion that I ordered the canoe to be set adrift, and gave the man the presents above mentioned, that when your Highnesses send another expedition to these parts it may meet with a friendly reception. All I gave the man was not worth four maravedis. We set sail about ten o'clock, with the wind southeast and stood southerly for the island I mentioned above, which is a very large one, and where according to the account of the natives on board, there is much gold, the inhabitants wearing it in bracelets upon their arms, legs, and necks, as well as in their ears and at their noses. This island is nine leagues distant from Santa Maria in a westerly direction. This part of it extends from northwest, to southeast and appears to be twenty-eight leagues long, very level, without any mountains, like San Salvador and Santa Maria, having a good shore and not rocky, except a few ledges under water, which renders it necessary to anchor at some distance, although the water is very clear, and the bottom may be seen. Two shots of a lombarda from the land, the water is so deep that it cannot be sounded; this is the case in all these islands. They are all extremely verdant and fertile, with the air agreeable, and probably contain many things of which I am ignorant, not inclining to stay here, but visit other islands in search of gold. And considering the indications of it among the natives who wear it upon their arms and legs, and having ascertained that it is the true metal by showing them some pieces of it which I have with me, I cannot fail, with the help of our Lord, to find the place which produces it.

Being at sea, about midway between Santa Maria and the large island, which I name Fernandina, we met a man in a canoe going from Santa Maria to Fernandina; he had with him a piece of the bread which the natives make, as big as one's fist, a calabash of water, a quantity of reddish earth, pulverized and afterwards kneaded up, and some dried leaves which are in high value among them, for a quantity of it was brought to me at San Salvador; he had besides a little basket made after their fashion, containing some glass beads, and two blancas by all which I knew he had come from San Salvador, and had passed from thence to Santa Maria. He came to the ship and I caused him to be taken on board, as he requested it; we took his canoe also on board and took care of his things. I ordered him to be presented with bread and honey, and drink, and shall carry him to Fernandina and give him his property, that he may carry a good report of us, so that if it please our Lord when your Highnesses shall send again to these regions, those who arrive here may receive honor, and procure what the natives may be found to possess.

Tuesday, 16 October. Set sail from Santa Maria about noon, for Fernandina which appeared very large in the west; sailed all the day with calms, and could not arrive soon enough to view the shore and select a good anchorage, for great care must be taken in this particular, lest the anchors be lost. Beat up and down all night, and in the morning arrived at a village and anchored. This was the place to which the man whom we had picked up at sea had gone, when we set him on shore. He had given such a favorable account of us, that all night there were great numbers of canoes coming off to us, who brought us water and other things. I ordered each man to be presented with something, as strings of ten or a dozen glass beads apiece, and thongs of leather, all which they estimated highly; those which came on board I directed should be fed with molasses. At three o'clock, I sent the boat on shore for water; the natives with great good will directed the men where to find it, assisted them in carrying the casks full of it to the boat, and seemed to take great pleasure in serving us. This is a very large island, and I have resolved to coast it about, for as I understand, in, or near the island, there is a mine of gold. It is eight leagues west of Santa Maria, and the cape where we have arrived, and all this coast extends from north-northwest to south-southeast. I have seen twenty leagues of it, but not the end. Now, writing this, I set sail with a southerly wind to circumnavigate the island, and search till we can find Samoet, which is the island or city where the gold is, according to the account of those who come on board the ship, to which the relation of those of San Salvador and Santa Maria corresponds. These people are similar to those of the islands just mentioned, and have the same language and customs; with the exception that they appear somewhat more civilized, showing themselves more subtle in their dealings with us, bartering their cotton and other articles with more profit than the others had experienced. Here we saw cotton cloth, and perceived the people more decent, the women wearing a slight covering of cotton over the nudities. The island is verdant, level and fertile to a high degree; and I doubt not that grain is sowed and reaped the whole year round, as well as all other productions of the place. I saw many trees, very dissimilar to those of our country, and many of them had branches of different sorts upon the same trunk; and such a diversity was among them that it was the greatest wonder in the world to behold. Thus, for instance, one branch of a tree bore leaves like those of a cane, another branch of the same tree, leaves similar to those of the lentisk. In this manner a single tree bears five or six different kinds. Nor is this done by grafting, for that is a work of art, whereas these trees grow wild, and the natives take no care about them. They have no religion, and I believe that they would very readily become Christians, as they have a good understanding. Here the fish are so dissimilar to ours that it is wonderful. Some are shaped like dories, of the finest hues in the world, blue, yellow, red, and every other color, some variegated with a thousand different tints, so beautiful that no one on beholding them could fail to express the highest wonder and admiration. Here are also whales. Beasts, we saw none, nor any creatures on land save parrots and lizards, but a boy told me he saw a large snake. No sheep nor goats were seen, and although our stay here has been short, it being now noon, yet were there any, I could hardly have failed of seeing them. The circumnavigation of the island I shall describe afterward.

Wednesday, 17 October. At noon set sail from the village where we had anchored and watered. Kept on our course to sail round the island; the wind southwest and south. My intention was to follow the coast of the island to the southeast as it runs in that direction, being informed by the Indians I have on board, besides another whom I met with here, that in such a course I should meet with the island which they call Samoet, where gold is found. I was further informed by Martin Alonzo Pinzon, captain of the Pinta, on board of which I had sent three of the Indians, that he had been assured by one of them I might sail round the island much sooner by the northwest. Seeing that the wind would not enable me to proceed in the direction I first contemplated, and finding it favorable for the one thus recommended me, I steered to the northwest and arriving at the extremity of the island at two leagues' distance, I discovered a remarkable haven with two entrances, formed by an island at its mouth, both very narrow, the inside capacious enough for a hundred ships, were there sufficient depth of water. I thought it advisable to examine it, and therefore anchored outside, and went with the boats to sound it, but found the water shallow. As I had first imagined it to be the mouth of a river, I had directed the casks to be carried ashore for water, which being done we discovered eight or ten men who straightway came up to us, and directed us to a village in the neighborhood; I accordingly dispatched the crews thither in quest of water, part of them armed, and the rest with the casks, and the place being at some distance it detained me here a couple of hours. In the meantime I strayed about among the groves, which present the most enchanting sight ever witnessed, a degree of verdure prevailing like that of May in Andalusia, the trees as different from those of our country as day is from night, and the same may be said of the fruit, the weeds, the stones and everything else. A few of the trees, however, seemed to be of a species similar to some that are to be found in Castile, though still with a great dissimilarity, but the others so unlike, that it is impossible to find any resemblance in them to those of our land. The natives we found like those already described, as to personal appearance and manners, and naked like the rest. Whatever they possessed, they bartered for what we chose to give them. I saw a boy of the crew purchasing javelins of them with bits of platters and broken glass. Those who went for water informed me that they had entered their houses and found them very clean and neat, with beds and coverings of cotton nets. Their houses are all built in the shape of tents, with very high chimneys. None of the villages which I saw contained more than twelve or fifteen of them. Here it was remarked that the married women wore cotton breeches, but the younger females were without them, except a few who were as old as eighteen years. Dogs were seen of a large and small size, and one of the men had hanging at his nose a piece of gold half as big as a castellailo, with letters upon it. I endeavored to purchase it of them in order to ascertain what sort of money it was but they refused to part with it. Having taken our water on board, I set sail and proceeded northwest till I had surveyed the coast to the point where it begins to run from east to west. Here the Indians gave me to understand that this island was smaller than that of Samoet, and that I had better return in order to reach it the sooner. The wind died away, and then sprang up from the west-northwest which was contrary to the course we were pursuing, we therefore hove about and steered various courses through the night from east to south standing off from the land, the weather being cloudy and thick. It rained violently from midnight till near day, and the sky still remains clouded; we remain off the southeast part of the island, where I expect to anchor and stay till the weather grows clear, when I shall steer for the other islands I am in quest of. Every day that I have been in these Indies it has rained more or less. I assure your Highnesses that these lands are the most fertile, temperate, level and beautiful countries in the world.

Thursday, 18 October. As soon as the sky grew clear, we set sail and went as far round the island as we could, anchoring when we found it inconvenient to proceed. I did not, however, land. In the morning set sail again.

Friday, 19 October. In the morning we got under weigh, and I ordered the Pinta to steer east and southeast and the Nina south- southeast; proceeding myself to the southeast the other vessels

I directed to keep on the courses prescribed till noon, and then to rejoin me. Within three hours we descried an island to the east toward which we directed our course, and arrived all three, before noon, at the northern extremity, where a rocky islet and reef extend toward the North, with another between them and the main island. The Indians on board the ships called this island Saomete. I named it Isabela. It lies westerly from the island of Fernandina, and the coast extends from the islet twelve leagues, west, to a cape which I called Cabo Hermoso, it being a beautiful, round headland with a bold shore free from shoals. Part of the shore is rocky, but the rest of it, like most of the coast here, a sandy beach. Here we anchored till morning. This island is the most beautiful that I have yet seen, the trees in great number, flourishing and lofty; the land is higher than the other islands, and exhibits an eminence, which though it cannot be called a mountain, yet adds a beauty to its appearance, and gives an indication of streams of water in the interior. From this part toward the northeast is an extensive bay with many large and thick groves. I wished to anchor there, and land, that I might examine those delightful regions, but found the coast shoal, without a possibility of casting anchor except at a distance from the shore. The wind being favorable, I came to the Cape, which I named Hermoso, where I anchored today. This is so beautiful a place, as well as the neighboring regions, that I know not in which course to proceed first; my eyes are never tired with viewing such delightful verdure, and of a species so new and dissimilar to that of our country, and I have no doubt there are trees and herbs here which would be of great value in Spain, as dyeing materials, medicine, spicery, etc., but I am mortified that I have no acquaintance with them. Upon our arrival here we experienced the most sweet and delightful odor from the flowers or trees of the island. Tomorrow morning before we depart, I intend to land and see what can be found in the neighborhood. Here is no village, but farther within the island is one, where our Indians inform us we shall find the king, and that he has much gold. I shall penetrate so far as to reach the village and see or speak with the king, who, as they tell us, governs all these islands, and goes dressed, with a great deal of gold about him. I do not, however, give much credit to these accounts, as I understand the natives but imperfectly, and perceive them to be so poor that a trifling quantity of gold appears to them a great amount. This island appears to me to be a separate one from that of Saomete, and I even think there may be others between them. I am not solicitous to examine particularly everything here, which indeed could not be done in fifty years, because my desire is to make all possible discoveries, and return to your Highnesses, if it please our Lord, in April. But in truth, should I meet with gold or spices in great quantity, I shall remain till I collect as much as possible, and for this purpose I am proceeding solely in quest of them.

Saturday, 20 October. At sunrise we weighed anchor, and stood to the northeast and east along the south side of this island, which I named Isabela, and the cape where we anchored, Cabo de la Laguna; in this direction I expected from the account of our Indians to find the capital and king of the island. I found the coast very shallow, and offering every obstacle to our navigation, and perceiving that our course this way must be very circuitous, I determined to return to the westward. The wind failed us, and we were unable to get near the shore before night; and as it is very dangerous anchoring here in the dark, when it is impossible to discern among so many shoals and reefs whether the ground be suitable, I stood off and on all night. The other vessels came to anchor, having reached the shore in season. As was customary among us, they made signals to me to stand in and anchor, but I determined to remain at sea.

Sunday, 21 October. At 10 o'clock, we arrived at a cape of the island, and anchored, the other vessels in company. After having dispatched a meal, I went ashore, and found no habitation save a single house, and that without an occupant; we had no doubt that the people had fled in terror at our approach, as the house was completely furnished. I suffered nothing to be touched, and went with my captains and some of the crew to view the country. This island even exceeds the others in beauty and fertility. Groves of lofty and flourishing trees are abundant, as also large lakes, surrounded and overhung by the foliage, in a most enchanting manner. Everything looked as green as in April in Andalusia. The melody of the birds was so exquisite that one was never willing to part from the spot, and the flocks of parrots obscured the heavens. The diversity in the appearance of the feathered tribe from those of our country is extremely curious. A thousand different sorts of trees, with their fruit were to be met with, and of a wonderfully delicious odor. It was a great affliction to me to be ignorant of their natures, for I am very certain they are all valuable; specimens of them and of the plants I have preserved. Going round one of these lakes, I saw a snake, which we killed, and I have kept the skin for your Highnesses; upon being discovered he took to the water, whither we followed him, as it was not deep, and dispatched him with our lances; he was seven spans in length; I think there are many more such about here. I discovered also the aloe tree, and am determined to take on board the ship tomorrow, ten quintals of it, as I am told it is valuable. While we were in search of some good water, we came upon a village of the natives about half a league from the place where the ships lay; the inhabitants on discovering us abandoned their houses, and took to flight, carrying of their goods to the mountain. I ordered that nothing which they had left should be taken, not even the value of a pin. Presently we saw several of the natives advancing towards our party, and one of them came up to us, to whom we gave some hawk's bells and glass beads, with which he was delighted. We asked him in return, for water, and after I had gone on board the ship, the natives came down to the shore with their calabashes full, and showed great pleasure in presenting us with it. I ordered more glass beads to be given them, and they promised to return the next day. It is my wish to fill all the water casks of the ships at this place, which being executed, I shall depart immediately, if the weather serve, and sail round the island, till I succeed in meeting with the king, in order to see if I can acquire any of the gold, which I hear he possesses. Afterwards I shall set sail for another very large island which I believe to be Cipango, according to the indications I receive from the Indians on board. They call the Island Colba, and say there are many large ships, and sailors there. This other island they name Bosio, and inform me that it is very large; the others which lie in our course, I shall examine on the passage, and according as I find gold or spices in abundance, I shall determine what to do; at all events I am determined to proceed on to the continent, and visit the city of Guisay, where I shall deliver the letters of your Highnesses to the Great Can, and demand an answer, with which I shall return.

Cortes's Second Letter to Charles V

In his "Second Letter" to Charles V, dated October 30, 1520, Cortés provides perhaps the most descriptive firsthand account of Tenochtitlan and the Aztec people:

IN ORDER, most potent Sire, to convey to your Majesty a just conception of the great extent of this noble city of Temixtitlan, and of the many rare and wonderful objects it contains; of the government and dominions of Moctezuma, the sovereign: of the religious rights and customs that prevail, and the order that exists in this as well as the other cities appertaining to his realm: it would require the labor of many accomplished writers, and much time for the completion of the task. I shall not be able to relate an hundredth part of what could be told respecting these matters; but I will endeavor to describe, in the best manner in my power, what I have myself seen; and imperfectly as I may succeed in the attempt, I am fully aware that the account will appear so wonderful as to be deemed scarcely worthy of credit; since even we who have seen these things with our own eyes, are yet so amazed as to be unable to comprehend their reality. But your Majesty may be assured that if there is any fault in my relation, either in regard to the present subject, or to any other matters of which I shall give your Majesty an account, it will arise from too great brevity rather than extravagance or prolixity in the details; and it seems to me but just to my Prince and Sovereign to declare the truth in the clearest manner, without saying anything that would detract from it, or add to it.

Before I begin to describe this great city and the others already mentioned, it may be well for the better understanding of the subject to say something of the configuration of Mexico, in which they are situated, it being the principal seat of Moctezuma's power. This Province is in the form of a circle, surrounded on all sides by lofty and rugged mountains; its level surface comprises an area of about seventy leagues in circumference, including two lakes, that overspread nearly the whole valley, being navigated by boats more than fifty leagues round. One of these lakes contains fresh and the other, which is the larger of the two, salt water. On one side of the lakes, in the middle of the valley, a range of highlands divides them from one another, with the exception of a narrow strait which lies between the highlands and the lofty sierras. This strait is a bow-shot wide, and connects the two lakes; and by this means a trade is carried on between the cities and other settlements on the lakes in canoes without the necessity of traveling by land. As the salt lake rises and falls with its tides like the sea, during the time of high water it pours into the other lake with the rapidity of a powerful stream; and on the other hand, when the tide has ebbed, the water runs from the fresh into the salt lake.

This great city of Temixtitlan [Mexico] is situated in this salt lake, and from the main land to the denser parts of it, by whichever route one chooses to enter, the distance is two leagues. There are four avenues or entrances to the city, all of which are formed by artificial causeways, two spears' length in width. The city is as large as Seville or

Cordova; its streets, I speak of the principal ones, are very wide and straight; some of these, and all the inferior ones, are half land and half water, and are navigated by canoes. All the streets at intervals have openings, through which the water flows, crossing from one street to another; and at these openings, some of which are very wide, there are also very wide bridges, composed of large pieces of timber, of great strength and well put together; on many of these bridges ten horses can go abreast. Foreseeing that if the inhabitants of the city should prove treacherous, they would possess great advantages from the manner in which the city is constructed, since by removing the bridges at the entrances, and abandoning the place, they could leave us to perish by famine without our being able to reach the main land, as soon as I had entered it, I made great haste to build four brigatines, which were soon finished, and were large enough to take ashore three hundred men and the horses, whenever it should become necessary.

This city has many public squares, in which are situated the markets and other places for buying and selling. There is one square twice as large as that of the city of Salamanca, surrounded by porticoes, where are daily assembled more than sixty thousand souls, engaged in buying and selling; and where are found all kinds of merchandise that the world affords, embracing the necessaries of life, as for instance articles of food, as well as jewels of gold and silver, lead, brass, copper, tin, precious stones, bones, shells, snails, and feathers. There are also exposed for sale wrought and unwrought stone, bricks burnt and unburnt, timber hewn and unhewn, of different sorts. There is a street for game, where every variety of birds in the country are sold, as fowls, partridges, quails, wild ducks, fly-catchers, widgeons, turtledoves, pigeons, reed-birds, parrots, sparrows, eagles, hawks, owls, and kestrels; they sell likewise the skins of some birds of prey, with their feathers, head, beak, and claws. There are also sold rabbits, hares, deer, and little dogs [i.e., the chihuahua], which are raised for eating. There is also an herb street, where may be obtained all sorts of roots and medicinal herbs that the country affords. There are apothecaries' shops, where prepared medicines, liquids, ointments, and plasters are sold; barbers' shops, where they wash and shave the head; and restaurateurs, that furnish food and drink at a certain price. There is also a class of men like those called in Castile porters, for carrying burdens. Wood and coal are seen in abundance, and braziers of earthenware for burning coals; mats of various kinds for beds, others of a lighter sort for seats, and for halls and bedrooms.

There are all kinds of green vegetables, especially onions, leeks, garlic, watercresses, nasturtium, borage, sorrel, artichokes, and golden thistle; fruits also of numerous descriptions, amongst which are cherries and plums, similar to those in Spain; honey and wax from bees, and from the stalks of maize, which are as sweet as the sugar-cane; honey is also extracted from the plant called maguey, which is superior to sweet or new wine; from the same plant they extract sugar and wine, which they also sell. Different kinds of cotton thread of all colors in skeins are exposed for sale in one quarter of the market, which has the appearance of the silk-market at Granada, although the former is supplied more abundantly. Painters' colors, as numerous as can be found in Spain, and as fine shades; deerskins dressed and undressed, dyed different colors; earthen-ware of a large size and excellent quality; large and small jars, jugs, pots, bricks, and endless variety of vessels, all made of fine clay, and all or most of them glazed and painted; maize or Indian corn, in the grain and in the form of bread, preferred in the grain for its flavor to that of the other islands and terra-firma; patés of birds and fish; great quantities of fish---fresh, salt, cooked and uncooked; the eggs of hens, geese, and of all the other birds I have mentioned, in great abundance, and cakes made of eggs; finally, everything that can be found throughout the whole country is sold in the markets, comprising articles so numerous that to avoid prolixity, and because their names are not retained in my memory, or are unknown to me, I shall not attempt to enumerate them.

Every kind of merchandise is sold in a particular street or quarter assigned to it exclusively, and thus the best order is preserved. They sell everything by number or measure; at least so far we have not observed them to sell anything by weight. There is a building in the great square that is used as an audience house, where ten or twelve persons, who are magistrates, sit and decide all controversies that arise in the market, and order delinquents to be punished. In the same square there are other persons who go constantly about among the people observing what is sold, and the measures used in selling; and they have been seen to break measures that were not true.

This great city contains a large number of temples, or houses, for their idols, very handsome edifices, which are situated in the different districts and the suburbs; in the principal ones religious persons of each particular sect are constantly residing, for whose use, besides the houses containing the idols, there are other convenient habitations. All these persons dress in black, and never cut or comb their hair from the time they enter the priesthood until they leave it; and all the sons of the principal inhabitants, both nobles and respectable citizens, are placed in the temples and wear the same dress from the age of seven or eight years until they are taken out to be married; which occurs more frequently with the first-born who inherit estates than with the others. The priests are debarred from female society, nor is any woman permitted to enter the religious houses. They also abstain from eating certain kinds of food, more at some seasons of the year than others.

Among these temples there is one which far surpasses all the rest, whose grandeur of architectural details no human tongue is able to describe; for within its precincts, surrounded by a lofty wall, there is room enough for a town of five hundred families. Around the interior of the enclosure there are handsome edifices, containing large halls and corridors, in which the religious persons attached to the temple reside. There are fully forty towers, which are lofty and well built, the largest of which has fifty steps leading to its main body, and is higher than the tower of the principal tower of the church at Seville. The stone and wood of which they are constructed are so well wrought in every part, that nothing could be better done, for the interior of the chapels containing the idols consists of curious imagery, wrought in stone, with plaster ceilings, and wood-work carved in relief, and painted with figures of monsters and other objects. All these towers are the burial places of the nobles, and every chapel in them is dedicated to a particular idol, to which they pay their devotions.

Three halls are in this grand temple, which contain the principal idols; these are of wonderful extent and height, and admirable workmanship, adorned with figures sculptured in stone and wood; leading from the halls are chapels with very small doors, to which the light is not admitted, nor are any persons except the priests, and not all of them. In these chapels are the images of idols, although, as I have before said, many of them are also found on the outside; the principal ones, in which the people have greatest faith and confidence, I precipitated from their pedestals, and cast them down the steps of the temple, purifying the chapels in which they had stood, as they were all polluted with human blood, shed ill the sacrifices. In the place of these I put images of Our Lady and the Saints, which excited not a little feeling in Moctezuma and the inhabitants, who at first remonstrated, declaring that if my proceedings were known throughout the country, the people would rise against me; for they believed that their idols bestowed on them all temporal good, and if they permitted them to be ill-treated, they would be angry and without their gifts, and by this means the people would be deprived of the fruits of the earth and perish with famine. I answered, through the interpreters, that they were deceived in expecting any favors from idols, the work of their own hands, formed of unclean things; and that they must learn there was but one God, the universal Lord of all, who had created the heavens and earth, and all things else, and had made them and us; that He was without beginning and immortal, and they were bound to adore and believe Him, and no other creature or thing.

I said everything to them I could to divert them from their idolatries, and draw them to a knowledge of God our Lord. Moctezuma replied, the others assenting to what he said, That they had already informed me they were not the aborigines of the country, but that their ancestors had emigrated to it many years ago; and they fully believed that after so long an absence from their native land, they might have fallen into some errors; that I having more recently arrived must know better than themselves what they ought to believe; and that if I would instruct them in these matters, and make them understand the true faith, they would follow my directions, as being for the best.@ Afterwards, Moctezuma and many of the principal citizens remained with me until I had removed the idols, purified the chapels, and placed the images in them, manifesting apparent pleasure; and I forbade them sacrificing human beings to their idols as they had been accustomed to do; because, besides being abhorrent in the sight of God, your sacred Majesty had prohibited it by law, and commanded to put to death whoever should take the life of another. Thus, from that time, they refrained from the practice, and during the whole period of my abode in that city, they were never seen to kill or sacrifice a human being.

The figures of the idols in which these people believe surpass in stature a person of more than ordinary size; some of them are composed of a mass of seeds and leguminous plants, such as are used for food, ground and mixed together, and kneaded with the blood of human hearts taken from the breasts of living persons, from which a paste is formed in a sufficient quantity to form large statues. When these are completed they make them offerings of the hearts of other victims, which they sacrifice to them, and besmear their faces with the blood. For everything they have an idol, consecrated by the use of the nations that in ancient times honored the same gods. Thus they have an idol that they petition for victory in war; another for success in their labors; and so for everything in which they seek or desire prosperity, they have their idols, which they honor and serve.

This noble city contains many fine and magnificent houses; which may be accounted for from the fact, that all the nobility of the country, who are the vassals of Moctezuma, have houses in the city, in which they reside a certain part of the year; and besides, there are numerous wealthy citizens who also possess fine houses. All these persons, in addition to the large and spacious apartments for ordinary purposes, have others, both upper and lower, that contain conservatories of flowers. Along one of these causeways that lead into the city are laid two pipes, constructed of masonry, each of which is two paces in width, and about five feet in height. An abundant supply of excellent water, forming a volume equal in bulk to the human body, is conveyed by one of these pipes, and distributed about the city, where it is used by the inhabitants for drink and other purposes. The other pipe, in the meantime, is kept empty until the former requires to be cleansed, when the water is let into it and continues to be used till the cleaning is finished. As the water is necessarily carried over bridges on account of the salt water crossing its route, reservoirs resembling canals are constructed on the bridges, through which the fresh water is conveyed. These reservoirs are of the breadth of the body of an ox, and of the same length as the bridges. The whole city is thus served with water, which they carry in canoes through all the streets for sale, taking it from the aqueduct in the following manner: the canoes pass under the bridges on which the reservoirs are placed, when men stationed above fill them with water, for which service they are paid. At all the entrances of the city, and in those parts where the canoes are discharged, that is, where the greatest quantity of provisions is brought in, huts are erected, and persons stationed as guards, who receive a certain sum of everything that enters. I know not whether the sovereign receives this duty or the city, as I have not yet been informed; but I believe that it appertains to the sovereign, as in the markets of other provinces a tax is collected for the benefit of the cacique.

In all the markets and public places of this city are seen daily many laborers waiting for some one to hire them. The inhabitants of this city pay a greater regard to style in their mode of dress and politeness of manners than those of the other provinces and cities; since, as the Cacique Moctezuma has his residence in the capital, and all the nobility, his vassals, are in constant habit of meeting there, a general courtesy of demeanor necessarily prevails. But not to be prolix in describing what relates to the affairs of this great city, although it is with difficulty I refrain from proceeding, I will say no more than that the manners of the people, as shown in their intercourse with one another, are marked by as great an attention to the proprieties of life as in Spain, and good order is equally well observed; and considering that they are barbarous people, without the knowledge of God, having no intercourse with civilized nations, these traits of character are worthy of admiration.

In regard to the domestic appointments of Moctezuma, and the wonderful grandeur and state that he maintains, there is so much to be told, that I assure your Highness I know not where to begin my relation, so as to be able to finish any part of it. For, as I have already stated, what can be more wonderful than a barbarous monarch, as he is, should have every object found in his dominions imitated in gold, silver, precious stones, and feathers; the gold and silver being wrought so naturally as not to be surpassed by any smith in the world; the stone work executed with such perfection that it is difficult to conceive what instruments could have been used; and the feather work superior to the finest productions in wax or embroidery. The extent of Moctezuma's dominions has not been ascertained, since to whatever point he despatched his messengers, even two hundred leagues from his capital, his commands were obeyed, although some of his provinces were in the midst of countries with which he was at war. But as nearly as I have been able to learn, his territories are equal in extent to Spain itself, for he sent messengers to the inhabitants of a city called Cumatan (requiring them to become subjects of your Majesty), which is sixty leagues beyond that part of Putunchan watered by the river Grijalva, and two hundred and thirty leagues distant from the great city; and I sent some of our people a distance of one hundred and fifty leagues in the same direction.

All the principle chiefs of these provinces, especially those in the vicinity of the capital, reside, as I have already stated, the greater part of the year in that great city, and all or most of them have their oldest sons in the service of Moctezuma. There are fortified places in all the provinces, garrisoned with his own men, where are also stationed his governors and collectors of the rents and tribute, rendered him by every province; and an account is kept of what each is obliged to pay, as they have characters and figures made on paper that are used for this purpose. Each province renders a tribute of its own peculiar productions, so that the sovereign receives a great variety of articles from different quarters. No prince was ever more feared by his subjects, both in his presence and absence. He possessed out of the city as well as within numerous villas, each of which had its peculiar sources of amusement, and all were constructed in the best possible manner for the use of a great prince and lord. Within the city his palaces were so wonderful that it is hardly possible to describe their beauty and extent; I can only say that in Spain there is nothing equal to them.

There was one palace somewhat inferior to the rest, attached to which was a beautiful garden with balconies extending over it, supported by marble columns, and having a floor formed of jasper elegantly inlaid. There were apartments in this palace sufficient to lodge two princes of the highest rank with their retinues. There were likewise belonging to it ten pools of water, in which were kept the different species of water birds found in this country, of which there is a great variety, all of which are domesticated; for the sea birds there were pools of salt water, and for the river birds, of fresh water. The water is let off at certain times to keep it pure, and is replenished by means of pipes. Each specie of bird is supplied with the food natural to it, which it feeds upon when wild. Thus fish is given to the birds that usually eat it; worms, maize, and the finer seeds, to such as prefer them. And I assure your Highness, that to the birds accustomed to eat fish there is given the enormous quantity of ten arrobas every day, taken in the salt lake. The emperor has three hundred men whose sole employment is to take care of these birds; and there are others whose only business is to attend to the birds that are in bad health.

Over the polls for the birds there are corridors and galleries, to which Moctezuma resorts, and from which he can look out and amuse himself with the sight of them. There is an apartment in the same palace in which are men, women and children, whose faces, bodies, hair, eyebrows, and eyelashes are white from their birth. The emperor has another very beautiful palace, with a large court-yard, paved with handsome flags, in the style of a chess-board. There are also cages, about nine feet in height and six paces square, each of which was half covered with a roof of tiles, and the other half had over it a wooden grate, skillfully made. Every cage contained a bird of prey, of all the species found in Spain, from the kestrel to the eagle, and many unknown there. There was a great number of each kind; and in the covered part of the cages there was a perch, and another on the outside of the grating, the former of which the birds used in the night time, and when it rained; and the other enabled them to enjoy the sun and air. To all these birds fowls were daily given for food, and nothing else. There were in the same palace several large halls on the ground floor, filled with immense cages built of heavy pieces of timber, well put together, in all or most of which were kept lions, tigers, wolves, foxes, and a variety of animals of the cat kind, in great numbers, which were fed also on fowls. The care of these animals and birds was assigned to three hundred men. There was another palace that contained a number of men and women of monstrous size, and also dwarfs, and crooked and ill-formed persons, each of which had their separate apartments. These also had their respective keepers. As to the other remarkable things that the emperor had in his city for his amusement, I can only say that they were numerous and of various kinds.

He was served in the following manner: Every day as soon as it was light, six hundred nobles and men of rank were in attendance at the palace, who either sat, or walked about the halls and galleries, and passed their time in conversation, but without entering the apartment where his person was. The servants and attendants of these nobles remained in the court-yards, of which there were two or three of great extent, and in the adjoining street, which was also very spacious. They all remained in attendance from morning until night; and when his meals were served, the nobles were likewise served with equal profusion, and their servants and secretaries also had their allowance. Daily his larder and wine-cellar were open to all who wished to eat or drink. The meals were served by three or four hundred youths, who brought on an infinite variety of dishes; indeed, whenever he dined or supped, the table was loaded with every kind of flesh, fish, fruits, and vegetables that the country produced. As the climate is cold, they put a chafing-dish with live coals under every plate and dish, to keep them warm. The meals were served in a large hall, in which Moctezuma was accustomed to eat, and the dishes quite filled the room, which was covered with mats and kept very clean. He sat on a small cushion curiously wrought of leather. During the meals there were present, at a little distance from him, five or six elderly caciques, to whom he presented some of the food. And there was constantly in attendance one of the servants, who arranged and handed the dishes, and who received from others whatever was wanted for the supply of the table.

Both at the beginning and end of every meal, they furnished water for the hands; and the napkins used on these occasions were never used a second time; this was the case also with the plates and dishes, which were not brought again, but new ones in place of them; it was the same also with the chafing-dishes. He is also dressed every day in four different suits, entirely new, which he never wears a second time. None of the caciques who enter his palace have their feet covered, and when those for whom he sends enters his presence, they incline their heads and look down, bending their bodies; and when they address him, they do not look him in the face; this arises from excessive modesty and reverence. I am satisfied that it proceeds from respect, since certain caciques reproved the Spaniards for their boldness in addressing me, saying that it showed a want of becoming deference. Whenever Moctezuma appeared in public, which is seldom the case, all those who accompanied him, or whom he accidentally met in the streets, turned away without looking towards him, and others prostrated themselves until he had passed. One of the nobles always preceded him on these occasions, carrying three slender rods erect, which I suppose was to give notice of the approach of his person. And when they descended from the litters, he took one of them in his hand, and held it until he reached the place where he was going. So many and various were the ceremonies and customs observed by those in the service of Moctezuma, that more space than I can spare would be required for the details, as well as a better memory than I have to recollect them; since no sultan or other infidel lord, of whom any knowledge now exists; ever had so much ceremonial in his court.

Bibliography

Beezley, William, and Michael C. Meyer. *The Oxford History of Mexico*. Oxford: Oxford University Press, 2010.

Díaz del Castillo, Bernal. *True and Full Account of the Conquest of Mexico and New Spain*. Trans. James Lockhart. Gutenberg Project Ebook.

Elliott, J.H. *The Old World and the New*. Cambridge: Cambridge University Press, 1992.

Pastor, Beatriz. *The Armature of Conquest: Spanish Accounts of the Discovery of America 1492-*

1589. Stanford: Stanford University Press, 1992.

Restall, Matthew. *Seven Myths of the Spanish Conquest*. Oxford: Oxford University Press, 2004.

37679795R00071

Made in the USA
Lexington, KY
12 December 2014